THE BROKER'S PRACTICAL GUIDE TO COMMERCIAL LEASING

SIDNEY G. SALTZ

Library of Congress Cataloging-in-Publication Data

Saltz, Sidney G., author.
  The broker's guide to commercial leasing / Sidney G. Saltz.
      pages cm
  Includes bibliographical references and index.
  ISBN 978-1-62722-294-5 (alk. paper)
  1. Commercial leases—United States. I. Title.
  KF593.C6S35 2013
  346.7304'3462—dc23

                                                    2013044200

Contents

Preface

I would like to start by giving some information about myself, about my experience, and why I am writing this book.

I am a general commercial real estate lawyer, practicing in the field for over 40 years. I have handled all kinds of transactions, including purchases and sales, financing, project development, and leasing. Leasing is a special love of mine as I have represented landlords or tenants in connection with ground leases, industrial/warehouse, office, retail and ground leases. I have been active for many years in the Real Property, Trust and Estate Section of the American Bar Association, chairing committees in the Leasing Group and also serving a two-year term as chair of the Leasing Group. I have also written extensively about leases in various journals and have lectured on the subject at many programs, including programs offered by the Society of Industrial and Office Realtors. I invite you to find out more about me and my practice by seeking out my website, www.sgsaltz.com.

In 2010, the American Bar Association published the second edition of my book *From Handshake to Closing—The Role of the Commercial Real Estate Lawyer*. It is a primer, principally for young lawyers and to assist in the training of law students about the practice of real estate law. That book contains a section on the role of the broker in commercial real estate transactions, and throughout the book the lawyer is encouraged to consult with the broker involved in the deal to resolve issues that arise during the course of the negotiations.

Unfortunately, the relationship between lawyers and brokers in real estate deals has not always been cordial. Often, brokers view lawyers as deal killers, and many lawyers think that brokers are only interested in getting the transaction done quickly so that they may collect their commission. While those perceptions may prove true on occasion, like most stereotypes, they should be approached with skepticism. The roles of the lawyer and the broker will be discussed in some detail below.

In doing a lease transaction, the broker must consider many issues other than the contents of the leasing document. Some of those issues will be discussed in this book. Then I will address various lease provisions that are usually found in all leases, whether they are industrial/warehouse, office, or retail. I will also consider how leases in each category may differ, based on the physical situation and the nature of the deal. Finally, I will discuss provisions unique to leases pertaining to each of those uses.

As I mentioned above, I spoke at programs presented by the Society of Industrial and Office Realtors. Actually, my client and friend, Steve Podolsky, and I taught the SIOR course on leases all over the country for over 20 years. I also worked with him extensively for many years as his attorney and for clients he referred to me and as to which he was serving as the broker. In all those situations, I learned a great deal from Steve, and I hope he learned a lot from me. Teaching that course with him, representing him, and working with him have helped me immensely in my practice, and are also the sources of many of the concepts discussed in this book, for which I am grateful. I am confident that Steve will forgive my appropriating his ideas (and sometimes his words) since Steve is a born teacher and has always been involved in educating brokers.

Steve contributed mightily by reviewing the manuscript for this book and making excellent suggestions for improvements. In addition, he is a consummate proofreader, and his edits have saved me from many embarrassing typographical errors.

In return for the use of his ideas, his suggested revisions, and his great proofreading, I am dedicating this book to him. I am also dedicating this book to my wife, Ann, a commercial leasing broker whom I met while teaching with Steve in Ft. Lauderdale, Florida, and who inspired me to write this in the first place.

PART I

INTRODUCTION

This Lawyer's Perception of What Leasing Brokers Do

I am aware that a lot of effort by both the broker who represents the tenant (known as the "tenant rep broker") and the broker who represents the property (usually referred to as the "landlord's broker") goes into a lease deal before the parties even consider looking at the leasing document. Of course, both brokers must be familiar with the market to determine if the rent and other business terms are consistent with what is being offered for comparable premises.

The broker may be familiar with the lease form that the landlord uses and may even be familiar with the physical condition of the space from having worked on that landlord's properties before. Unless the tenant rep broker has represented tenants leasing from that landlord in the same property, he or she has a longer learning curve. In either case, that broker must understand the particular client's business to be able to evaluate whether the location, size, and amenities are appropriate. In the case of a retail facility, he or she must ascertain whether the location of the particular shopping center is conducive for attracting the type of clientele the client caters to and whether the parking is adequate. A restaurant or a grocery store needs a lot of parking, but a furniture store, which sells fewer but higher-priced items, needs less. A store in a shopping center will be concerned that a kiosk or other facility does not obstruct visibility. The prospective tenant might be concerned with existing competition and may need some sort of exclusivity to protect it from future competition. In the case of a warehouse building, the user may be concerned about the fire protection system. Will sprinklers ruin the merchandise, so that another type of system will be required? Is the ceiling height appropriate for the use? Will the tenant need space that allows trucks to drive in, load, and drive out the other end? Even office tenants have unique concerns. Is the adjoining tenant one with a lot of traffic, which will cause noise and possibly tie up the elevator? A medical tenant might need access to water and extra electric power.

In addition, the tenant rep broker must confirm that the physical condition of the premises will not create any problems when the client occupies them. This issue revolves around the nature of the physical structure and the proposed business to be conducted in the space. Needless to say, if office premises are in the middle of a relatively new high-rise building, there should not be much danger of a roof leak, but a single-story warehouse building or retail space might well be at risk. Thus, depending again on the circumstances, the tenant rep broker may encourage the client to perform physical due diligence, or arrange for due diligence inspections on the client's behalf, by obtaining some or all of the following:

1. general description of the property and of the neighborhood
2. building plans and specifications, if available
3. roof report
4. engineering reports to cover the following items:
   a. structure including the condition of the slab, columns, bumpers, structural walls, exterior doors, and dock doors
   b. masonry
   c. exterior caulking
   d. exterior painting
   e. washrooms and locker rooms
   f. interior ventilation
   g. unit heaters
   h. mechanical systems including sprinkler systems, electrical, plumbing, and heating, ventilating, and air-conditioning (HVAC)
   i. lighting, ceiling tiles and light lenses, dry wall, entrance steps
   j. compliance with laws and ordinances (including Americans with Disabilities Act)
   k. building size
   l. parking lot

    m.   landscaping
5. Phase I Environmental Assessment (including asbestos)
6. Phase II Environmental Assessment, if recommended by engineer
7. floor or space plans
8. warranties (including roof) and assignability thereof
9. meters in multi-tenant spaces
10. permits
11. soil analysis for load-bearing capacity, in the case of new construction
12. access and other appurtenant rights, such as easements that benefit the property
13. code violation search from the local municipality, if required
14. availability of utilities
15. loading docks
16. vermin infestation or bad odors

The tenant rep broker should do some due diligence dealing with the credit of the landlord, particularly if the landlord is performing leasehold or other improvements to the property, or is agreeing to pay a tenant allowance. He or she should also check the zoning to make certain that the proposed use complies. Landlords usually resist warranting the zoning, ostensibly because they claim not to be familiar with the nature of the tenant's use, but actually because the landlord does not want to take the risk of a breach that might give the tenant a right to terminate the lease or sue for the breach if the market turns sour.

Both brokers will negotiate the terms of the deal, with client input or participation, based on the respective needs of the parties. In addition to the basic concerns, such as rent and initial term, those may include term extension, early termination, expansion or contraction rights, build-out, responsibility for repairs, maintenance, and replacements, and a host of other matters customarily included in term sheets or letters of intent.

Once the parties agree on those basic terms and the prospective tenant is satisfied with the condition of the premises (or is confident that it will have the opportunity, before it is fully bound, to satisfy itself), the parties may often prepare and sign a letter of intent. Usually the lawyers for the parties will not see the letter of intent before it is signed. That may be a serious mistake.

Letters of Intent

When it comes to letters of intent, there are two questions to be considered. The first is, when are letters of intent binding? The second is, for what purpose? Are they binding for the purpose of creating an obligation to negotiate in good faith? Or are they binding as an agreement between the parties as to the terms and conditions of the transaction?

There are many judicial decisions dealing with letters of intent. Unfortunately, the answer to the questions may turn, in part, on the language in the letter of intent and in part on other evidence of the intent of the parties. In other words, even though there may be language in a letter of intent stating that it is not intended to bind the parties to an agreement until a final agreement is written up, executed, and delivered, the parties may in fact be bound. At the very least, a letter of intent may create an obligation to negotiate in good faith, unless that is expressly negated in the letter of intent.

Brokers like letters of intent. First, but not necessarily foremost, the letter of intent may result in the entitlement to a commission based on the broker having found a ready, willing, and able tenant for his or her client's space. More often, however, commissions are not really earned until a lease is signed, so that is not a major reason. No, brokers like letters of intent because they document the basic terms of the deal and facilitate the drafting of the lease. The letter of intent drafted by the broker may contain language that negates the intent to create a binding agreement, but that may not be entirely effective.

Often a broker representing a tenant will make a request for proposal (RFP) to the landlord or its broker and receive a detailed response, which will contain the business terms of the deal. Sometimes the broker will make an "offer," setting forth the terms on which the tenant or the landlord, as the case may be, is willing to enter into the lease. That offer may be "accepted" or may be subject to a "counteroffer." I put the words in quotation marks because the offers, acceptances, and counteroffers are not really intended to be used in the context of creating a binding agreement, and they probably do not do so for several reasons. First, it is understood in the trade that it is not their purpose. More importantly, the broker does not usually have the authority to bind a client to a lease. The actual parties do not customarily sign the papers being exchanged (unless, of course, there are no brokers involved). The problem really arises when the brokers take the terms that have been discussed, either orally or by RFP or offer and acceptance, and reduce them to writing in a letter of intent and ask the parties to sign them. Remember that, at this point in time, it is most likely that neither party has consulted its attorney.

Let us assume that I, as one of the party's attorneys, am consulted at that point in the process. Whether I represent the landlord or the tenant, my advice is do not sign! The parties, by signing, may create a binding agreement, even though important matters have not been dealt with, or have been dealt with in an imprecise manner. Even if the letter of intent is accurate and contains all sorts of language about not creating a binding lease, there may still be problems. The problems may be made worse by making the letter of intent very detailed. I have seen letters of intent that were extremely long and contained almost all of the terms of the agreement, using in many instances the very language contained in the lease proposed to be entered into. I do not believe that any amount of language stating that the letter of intent is not binding (except, perhaps, conditions such as approval by the party's governing body, such as a board of directors of a corporation or members of a limited liability company) could have kept that letter of intent from actually being enforced as the agreement between the parties.

What are some of the other problems with letters of intent?

While a major purpose of a letter of intent is to discourage each party from seeking a better deal before the current negotiations are wrapped up, some letters of intent actually require the landlord to stop marketing the property. The landlord's broker should strongly object to that provision because it places what I deem to be intolerable burdens on that party. It may have to incur the cost of removing large and expensive "For Rent" signs (and replacing them if the deal does not go through), but that is a minor matter compared with the requirement that the client turn away prospects or not seek a backup tenant when it does not have a firm deal. The problem is more serious when the tenant is to be afforded a period of time to conduct its due diligence or obtain zoning or permits, at the end of which period it may terminate the proposed deal, leaving the landlord with no alternative tenants.

In addition, a letter of intent may create an obligation to negotiate in good faith, and the refusal to agree to some important term may result in a claim (and litigation) that the party has failed to live up to that obligation. That puts particular pressure on the parties subsequently negotiating the lease, especially if, in the course of negotiation, issues are raised (and agreed to) that are inconsistent with the terms of the letter of intent. I experienced an example of that some years ago. A landlord client signed a letter of intent, which committed the landlord to forgo certain benefits. The tenant asked for a larger build-out allowance than was contemplated by the landlord (the issue was not clear in the letter of intent). The landlord granted the concession, but changed the lease to restore the benefits, and sent a redlined copy of the lease to the tenant, highlighting the change in the benefit language. The tenant actually signed the redlined copy of the lease (implying that it had reviewed the changes since the prior draft), but then sued the landlord, claiming that the lease did not accurately reflect the agreement of the parties. To avoid protracted litigation and expense, the landlord settled the case.

Under the circumstances, what do I recommend?

1. The actual parties to the deal should not sign letters of intent. I mean that in two senses. The parties should avoid using letters of intent. They will, however, probably use them because they have some advantages. In that case they should not sign them—nor should they give a written authorization to any third party to sign on their behalf, because they may be deemed to have complied with the Statute of Frauds and be bound by the terms of the letter of intent without intending to be.[1] There are alternatives to letters of intent that are far less dangerous. For example, I recommend using a term sheet. It states, in essence, that "the following are the terms on which the parties propose to

---

1. Most states have enacted the "Statute of Frauds," which provides that contracts for the sale of real estate and leases for a term in excess of one year must be signed by the party to be bound.

lease such and such property," and then only the basic terms are set out. It is always wise to provide that the document set out a date after which either party may terminate discussions without liability. It may even expressly negate an obligation to negotiate in good faith, if that is agreeable to the parties. Vagueness is the key. If the parties do not sign the letter of intent and the Statute of Frauds applies, the letter of intent does not bind the parties. There are two caveats. First, if a broker signs for a party, it should be clear that the broker is without written authority to bind the party. Second, beware of the federal Electronic Signatures in Global and National Commerce Act. A letter of intent sent via e-mail by a person who is employed by one of the parties and who has authority to sign a lease may satisfy the requirements of that act and bind the party.

2. If parties must use and sign a letter of intent, it should certainly contain the language negating the intent to create a binding agreement, despite the issues discussed above. If possible, conditions to the conclusion of a lease should be inserted, such as board approval, the tenant's confirmation of the zoning or condition of the premises (in its discretion), or the landlord's satisfaction (again in its discretion) with the tenant's financial condition or operation of its prior premises. If the obligation to negotiate in good faith is not negated in the language of the letter of intent, time periods should be provided for the delivery of the draft lease and for the completion of the negotiations, after which the parties will have no obligations under the letter of intent.

3. If you represent the landlord, recommend to your client that it not agree to take the space off the market until a lease is signed.

If you have a question about the letter of intent and its possible effect, you should ask your client if you may contact its lawyer to make certain that you do not fall into any of the traps I have described.

Enter the Lawyer

Yes, some lawyers are deal killers—but most are not. Some deals should be killed, especially if issues arise that are important to one of the parties and they cannot be satisfactorily resolved. In those situations, the broker should be as eager to protect the client as the lawyer is.

It is important to understand where the lawyer is coming from—and where the broker is coming from as well. Both parties have common goals: to enable the client to lease premises (either as the landlord or the tenant), but also to protect the client from making a bad deal.

The lawyer's role is the more conservative one. He or she is seeking to protect the client from risk. The lawyer drafting the lease and the lawyer reviewing the lease on behalf of the other party are both trying to anticipate all the bad things that might happen during the term of the lease and to make certain that their clients are not materially injured by those events.

The lawyers (other than in-house lawyers) are generally paid by the hour, although that is no longer universally true. And they are usually paid whether the lease is finalized or not. That makes brokers suspicious that the lawyer has no incentive to push the lease to fruition.

Brokers tend to be more entrepreneurial than lawyers. They are out there in the business world creating deals. Brokers are often (but not universally) paid on a contingent-fee basis—they are paid commissions if the lease is signed, but nothing if the deal dies. The commissions are often substantial, generally more substantial than the legal fees. That makes lawyers suspect that brokers are pushing the conclusion of the lease to get paid, without adequately protecting the interests of the client. The lawyer may be particularly suspicious of a broker in the situation of dual agency, in which different brokers in the same firm represent the landlord and the tenant, especially if the broker representing his or her client is a principal in the firm. Even though protections are built into that situation, the lawyer might feel that the particular broker working withthe lawyer's client may not be wholeheartedly representing that client.

While there can be no doubt that some lawyers are unprincipled enough to try to kill deals in order to get a second bite at fees, just as some brokers are willing to let the client sign an unfavorable lease just to get paid the commission or to ease up on the negotiations because another person in his or her firm is representing the other party. However, on further consideration, we can see that such unethical behavior is not in the interest of either professional. The lawyer's client will soon figure out that it did not get a much better deal on the subsequent lease and conclude that either the lawyer did not know what he or she was doing or that the handling of the matter was not appropriate. As to the broker, the client will also decide that the broker was not acting in its interest and, even if it may not cost the broker a commission on that deal, it may cost the broker future business with that client, and perhaps his or her reputation in the community.

The broker's relationship with lawyers, or a specific lawyer, may depend on whether the broker is working for the landlord or the tenant and on the nature of the work with the landlord or the tenant. Thus, if the broker is representing a landlord with numerous properties, a standard lease and a lawyer it deals with on all its leases, that broker will already have a method of operating with the lawyer and vice versa. Likewise, if a tenant has numerous locations and a standard lease form, the situation is pretty much set, except that the tenant may use different lawyers in different states. In the latter situation, although the broker may be familiar with the lease form, the broker may not be aware of particular local customs or laws and thus be required to work with an unfamiliar person. In a one-off situation, in which the landlord owns little or no other property and is not generally in the real estate business or the tenant is leasing a single location for the operation of its business, the relationship between the broker and the lawyer on the same side may become more tenuous or adversarial.

How does the broker's suspicion of lawyers affect the transaction? Well, the broker may discourage the client from using a lawyer at all. The broker may say, "This is a simple lease. I can negotiate it myself. I can even draft any necessary changes in the document."

I submit that such a course is very dangerous, not only for the client but for the broker as well. Let me propose a hypothetical situation.

A tenant rep broker receives the lease draft from the landlord's representative and reviews it. Leases are not as simple as they may look. In this hypothetical situation, the tenant is a restaurant and will be spending a lot of money on tenant improvements. The lease provides for subordination (which will be discussed starting on page 41), but the broker, who does not have much experience or expertise, considers it legal mumbo jumbo and skips over it. The broker does notice some language that is not in accordance with the letter of intent or what he or she deems not to be in the best interest of the tenant, so he or she drafts alternative lease language.

The lease is signed and the first thing that happens during the term is that there is a dispute between the landlord and the tenant—and it happens to relate to the language the broker drafted. It seems that the language is ambiguous, which is not unusual. Unfortunately, the parties are unable to resolve the dispute and a lawsuit is filed. The judge is asked to determine what the language means. It being ambiguous, the judge cannot interpret the language. Since neither party really considered the issue when the lease was being negotiated, they cannot testify as to what was intended, so the judge takes recourse to a rule of construction to help decide the issue. That rule says that, in the case of ambiguous language, it is construed most strongly against the drafter. The tenant loses the lawsuit because its broker drafted the language on its behalf, so the tenant looks around for some way to recoup the loss resulting from the ambiguous drafting. Where does it look but to the drafter—the broker! And when the broker tries to collect on the errors and omissions (E&O) insurance, he or she will find out that the E&O insurance does not cover the unauthorized practice of law, which is exactly what happened here. The broker (or the broker's firm) will have to pay the tenant's loss out of its own pocket. Mark my words: drafting lease language constitutes the practice of law, and the practice of law by someone not admitted by the Supreme Court of the state to do so is illegal—probably even a criminal offense.

All right, the broker pays the loss and does not happen to be prosecuted for practicing law without a license. Is he or she out of the woods? Remember that other little twist? The one about the legal mumbo jumbo? Something about subordination? The next thing that happens to our poor tenant is that the landlord defaults under the mortgage and the lender files a foreclosure. The lender concludes that the broker's client got too good a deal (he or she did a good job on that one, or maybe the market has changed). So, in the foreclosure action, the lender names the tenant as a defendant and terminates the lease. There goes the profitable restaurant. There goes all the money spent on leasehold improvements. Our poor broker did not know about a thing called a non-disturbance agreement, where the lender agrees not to foreclose on the tenant. Guess who pays again, and big-time now.

It is certainly true that a lawyer may draft ambiguous language, too, or forget a non-disturbance agreement. I have seen it done. However, the lawyer can insure against his or her errors and omissions relative to the practice of law, and from the broker's point of view, "Better him than me!"

A situation may arise in which the client, desiring to save legal fees, asks the broker to review the lease and draft language. The broker should respectfully decline to do it. The client may even pressure the broker to undertake that task, but the broker should bear in mind the risk and tell the client that he or she is legally prohibited from practicing law and cannot undertake the task.

In Illinois, lawyers and brokers litigated over what constituted the unauthorized practice of law by brokers and settled the case by entering into a Broker-Lawyer Accord. It authorizes brokers to fill in the blanks in printed contract forms. This may work out fine in connection with the sales of homes or condominium apartments, but has little application to leasing. There may be blanks in the landlord's form, but those are the tip of the iceberg in leases. Of course, what may be determined to be unauthorized practice of law differs from state to state, and, in fact, the Illinois rule may be considered pretty liberal in favor of brokers. It was, after all, a settlement.

I have heard brokers say that they draft language and submit it to their attorney or the client's attorney for approval. I am sorry to inform you that, even if the lawyer approves it (and may create his or her own liability), it does not get the broker off the hook for unauthorized practice of law and also being held liable for bad consequences. I am not just trying to protect my turf; I am saying this for the broker's own protection.

The lawyer does not come out scot-free from his or her suspicion of the broker, either. Many lawyers think the broker should bring the deal to the lawyer and get out of the way, but that can have some bad effects for the lawyer. The problem is that the lawyer was not in on the deal from the get-go. He or she does not have the same feeling as the broker often does for the client's needs, an understanding of the market and that this deal may be the only reasonable choice for the client, and certainly the sense of the nuances of the prior negotiations. Of course, the lawyer can get a lot of information from the client, but if the client is not sophisticated in real estate matters, the information is likely to be partial, biased, or otherwise inadequate. The lawyer's best source of important information is the broker.

Another problem brokers confront with lawyers—and this is real and too common—is that many clients have lawyers who do not do real estate work as a part of their regular practice and really do not understand the nuances of the lease. In fact, those lawyers often focus on all the wrong issues and leave the tough problems unaddressed and unresolved. This is a very touchy situation for brokers, particularly when the lawyer is a relative of the client or even the client's in-house counsel. It may be that the least-experienced lawyer is also the one who is least likely to want to work with the broker, because the broker will quickly see that the lawyer is not up to the job. How does the broker deal with that one? Very gingerly! The client's relationship with the lawyer, even if he or she is not a relative, is probably a long-standing one that is based on trust and confidence. It's just that the lawyer—who won a big personal injury judgment for the client or wrote his estate plan or even the in-house guy who handled a major merger or acquisition—may not be not familiar with the intricacies of a lease. Some large companies with legal staffs simply may not want to spend money on outside counsel when they are paying good money for that staff. Still, the broker has a professional responsibility to tell the client that the lawyer does not have the required expertise. Of course, the broker risks alienating the client and will certainly create an enemy in the deal if the lawyer is not replaced (and an enemy if he or she is replaced). I cannot suggest words to use in that situation (which is not that uncommon), but the broker's duty to the client to be truthful and to represent the client's best interest dictates disclosure. It is important to consider and communicate the fact—and it is a fact—that a lawyer who does not have expertise in leasing is the true deal killer.

An experienced real estate lawyer brings a lot to the table. He or she probably has represented landlords in some deals, tenants in others, and even lenders from time to time. That lawyer will know what points to raise or how to respond to the points raised by his or her counterpart who represents the other party, knows what to concede and what to insist upon, and when and how to compromise (depending, of course, on the nature of the deal, the client's strengths or weaknesses, and the state of the market—as to which the broker's input is critical). He or she will not get bogged down arguing about matters that are not important or are not in the other party's interest to concede. If the lawyers on both sides are well qualified to negotiate the lease, the deal will move more quickly, cost less in legal fees, and result in fairer terms. If brokers are recommending that a client not use an inexperienced lawyer, they would be well advised to be in a position to recommend one or more lawyers who they know to have the expertise to represent the client fairly, efficiently, and expertly.[2]

How do you, the broker, manage to get together with the lawyer and work out a modus operandi? You may be lucky and the lawyer may call you to indicate a desire to work together. I would, and perhaps lawyers who have read my book, "From Handshake to Closing," would, but do not hold your breath! No, you will probably have to make the first move. You should e-mail or, preferably, call the lawyer, introduce yourself, and tell the lawyer that you represent the same client. Tell the lawyer you would like to receive a copy of the lease when it is prepared, that you plan to read it, and you would appreciate the opportunity to discuss it with him or her after that. You should also indicate that you would like to be included in any calls or meetings and receive e-mails pertaining to the negotiation of the lease. You should emphasize that you do not intend to encroach on his or her territory, but hope that you can be useful in providing input that will be helpful to your mutual client. It might also be a good idea to engage in some social chitchat, comparing whom you know and the like, to establish a sort of friendly relationship. It is important to remember that lawyers are always looking for referrals and if you indicate that you have clients who may need qualified legal representation, you may find that the lawyer will become quite friendly and amenable to working with you. And if the lawyer does in fact work with you and has confidence in your ability, he or she may even refer business to you. Lawyers are human too . . . at least usually.

It is critically important that the broker, and the lawyer, bear in mind at all times that, irrespective of the dynamic between them, it is the client who will bear the burdens and enjoy the benefits of the lease they are working to

---

2. In Illinois, under the Broker-Lawyer Accord, the broker must suggest three lawyers. That requirement may be different in other states.

finalize. For that reason, both of them must always defer to the client and not simply allow—but enable—the client to make all the ultimate decisions on the issues that affect those burdens and benefits.

In order to earn the confidence of the lawyer and make him or her willing to work with you on that particular deal and in the future, you must demonstrate that you understand the various provisions in the lease and are capable of making a useful contribution to the finalization of the deal.

This is where the rest of this book comes in. First, I shall discuss lease forms, then describe the various types of premises available for different users, and then discuss different uses in various types of leases and, in general, issues raised by each type. I will then describe and discuss lease provisions common to most types of leases. Finally, I will discuss provisions that apply particularly to each of the various types of lease. Bear in mind that, although I will write about lease provisions and the issues relating to those provisions, it is impossible to exhaustively cover all possible lease provisions and their problems. My purpose is to enable brokers to recognize issues in leases and to contribute to the resolution of those issues.

Lease Forms

Once the negotiation of the business terms has been concluded and a letter of intent has been signed or a term sheet agreed to, someone—usually the lawyer for the landlord, but sometimes the one for the tenant—will pull out his or her lease form and put the business terms, as he or she understands them, into that form. There are, of course, different lease forms for various lease situations.

Lease forms come in many sizes and degrees of complexity and readability. Some are well drafted, some are not. If you regularly represent a landlord, or even a tenant who has the clout to insist that its lease form be used, you , as the tenant rep broker, may have input into the form of lease used. More often, however, you will be presented with a lease form that you may have never seen before.

Where do lease forms come from? They usually come from prior lease forms. A lawyer starting out in leasing will seek out a form drafted by someone else—either a person in his or her firm, or from a form book, of which there are many in printed or electronic form. The lawyer might then make changes in the lease form, trying to bring it up to date and to deal with changes in the law. For example, before there were environmental laws, there were, of course, very few leases that dealt with pollution. Certainly lease forms have been modified to deal with that issue. The enactment of the ADA required more modifications. Another reason lease forms change is that a client may have encountered problems because some language was included or not included in the lease form. For example, I was once involved in an industrial lease situation in which the tenant's use caused corrosion of the heating equipment. When the landlord advised the tenant that it would have to replace the equipment at the end of the term, the tenant rather cleverly took the position that the corrosion was an inevitable result of the permitted use, of which the landlord had full knowledge, and thus was reasonable wear and tear. The client told me to change the form to add language "so that never happens to me again"—and I did.

Lease forms change as a result of lawyers reviewing provisions in other lawyers' leases that the reviewing lawyer feels should be included in his or her form, so the lawyer cuts and pastes the language into the form. Sometimes it is easy to spot the insertion because suddenly the landlord and the tenant are being referred to as the lessor and the lessee, or the insertion is inconsistent with other provisions in the lease form. Often a lawyer using his or her own lease form simply notices provisions that could be better drafted and so makes the change.

Some lease forms are well drafted and some are not. Some are up to date and some are archaic. The problem is that lawyers, for lack of time, lack of knowledge, or lack of interest, often do not give enough consideration to their lease forms, which tend to become overly long, unduly legalistic, and internally inconsistent. This makes many leases hard to read and hard to negotiate, especially since the lawyer who drafted the lease may have a certain pride of authorship (even if that pride is not warranted) or because the lawyer is not sufficiently experienced to understand the shortcomings of the form. Those forms—all leases, in fact—call for careful and concentrated review, a good relationship with your client's attorney, as well as finesse in negotiation, to get the form (and more importantly, the deal) to where it should be (or should have been in the first place).

Types of Premises

People who deal in or have an interest in real estate generally think in terms of three basic types of premises: industrial/warehouse, office, and retail. Many would also add to the basic types vacant land and land with a building to be demolished.[3] Actually, the selection of types of premises is much more diverse and complicated.

In the industrial/warehouse scenario, the premises may be an entire building or in a multi-tenant building. They may be in a single building or in part of an industrial park (now customarily called by fancier names like "business complex"). They might even be part of a larger complex of commercial uses, including office, retail, or even some residential. They may be located near an airport, or in an area that had or continues to have heavy industrial uses or one that was previously totally undeveloped.

The office situation may be even more diverse. The premises may be in a single-tenant, single-story building; a multi-tenant, single-story building; a single-tenant, multistory building; a multi-tenant, multistory building; or a multiuse building with retail on the lower floors. Some buildings even have residences on the upper floors. The building might have general-use office space only or it may include or be exclusively for medical use. It may be located in the central business district, suburbia, or even exurbia.

Retail is also very diverse. The space to be leased may be located in a regional mall, a community shopping center, a strip mall, or a multiuse building (including office and/or residential). It may be freestanding. It may be a multistory department store, a big box, a supermarket—every shape or size, down to the mom-and-pop neighborhood food store or barbershop. It may be located in a central business district, on an upscale retail street, in a suburb, on a commercial street, or even in a residential neighborhood.

---

3. Agricultural and mineral leases, although important, are not within the scope of this book.

Vacant land or a building to be demolished may be located anywhere and be of any size.

Of course, you know all of this. You see it all around you. I just discuss this to highlight what follows next: the discussion of different uses and different lease situations.

Different Uses and Lease Situations

Industrial/Warehouse Leases
Uses

The uses to which this type of property may be put is as varied as American industry. They may include heavy manufacturing, although I suspect most companies that operate that type of plant own their own facilities. For the leasing broker, most leases involving manufacturing will be for light manufacturing or assembly. Still, those uses can present substantial problems for owners. For example, the use or repackaging of chemicals may create environmental problems or be corrosive to the space and the roof (depending on how the fumes are ventilated) or to the HVAC systems. A food-processing facility may create odor or vermin issues or use a lot of water, which can affect the finished surface of the floor. I recall a situation in which a seafood processor in a multi-tenant building promised that his operation was clean and did not create uncontrolled odors and that in fact, the landlord checked out its prior facility before leasing to it. However, it turned out not to be true, and the adjoining tenants complained bitterly about the smell. Fortunately, the lease prohibited odor problems, and the landlord could evict the tenant. Unfortunately, the odor had entered into the cinder block, demising walls, and continued to be a problem for an extended period of time.

Heavy equipment may damage the floor. The bearing capacity of the floor will have to be determined before leasing to a user that has heavy equipment. The user may have to dig a pit in the floor to operate equipment. Provisions will have to be made in the lease for the restoration of the floor to its original condition. A use may require a great deal of electricity and conduit or bus duct running in places that may be inconvenient for a subsequent user, or that may be useful to the next user but bring up an issue of ownership.

I worked on a lease in which the tenant was a bread bakery. Its operation required very prompt delivery of its products to maintain freshness. That was to be accomplished by having trucks drive into the premises on one side, be loaded, and then drive out the other side. The tenant required street-level truck entry and exit and truck doors at either end of the premises. Needless to say, not many users need a configuration like that, so the landlord required a large security deposit to pay for the restoration of the opposite wall. The tenant argued that it should not be required to pay for restoration at the end of the lease because the landlord might find another user who would require in-and-out truck doors. Although that was like the needle in the haystack, the landlord in that case agreed to market the premises for such a use before the expiration of the lease and for a short time afterward, but if it was not successful, or if it leased the premises for another use, the security deposit was to be applied for its intended purpose.

A user might require the right to install an overhead crane. That creates a weight issue and a serious removal issue, which will have to be dealt with in the negotiation and documentation of the lease.

Of course, a lot of the same issues may apply in connection with a warehouse. The stinky fish operator may have been storing the fish, not processing it, and the drive-through building may have been used by a beer distributor instead of a bakery. Also, even a light manufacturer or assembler may very likely be using a portion of its premises for warehousing its products.

An important aspect of the suitability of proposed premises is the clear space, which is the dimension between floor and the underside of the sprinkler heads or the lights, whichever is lower. If the tenant's business is a pick-and-pack kind of operation, such as a pharmaceutical supply house (where the employees move through the warehouse and pick the items on their lists off of shelves), the merchandise must be accessible without the picker having to climb a lot of ladders. Less clear space is then desirable, since more clear space would be expensive to lease and to heat or cool, but wasted. On the other hand, massive containers of merchandise that are to be shipped in those containers need a lot of clear space. Attention must also be paid to the type of fire protection on the premises. A water-based system could be a disaster for the pharmaceutical supply house or a warehouse that stores newsprint, but not a problem for a user who stores merchandise in waterproof containers.

It is the responsibility of the brokers for both parties to become familiar with the details of the proposed use, and also of the ability of the proposed premises to meet the requirements of the prospective tenant. For example, if the parking lot cannot sustain the weight of large trucks or the configuration of the docks does not allow semis to back into them, the proposed premises will not work for some tenants. It is particularly the responsibility each of the parties brokers to make certain that the zoning does not prohibit the proposed use in that location, or require a variance or special-use permit from the municipality, and that if there is to be construction, the physical requirements, such as those relating to setbacks and automobile and truck parking, can be met by the tenant. It does no good to pursue a lease for drive-through premises if the opposite wall of the premises cannot structurally support further openings, for example, or if the zoning does not permit two such driveways. If the use may create additional costs for the landlord at the end of the term, those costs should be dealt with in negotiation and documentation of the lease, and consideration should be given to securing the obligation to pay those costs. In fact, all the special-use issues should be considered as part of the viewing of premises and negotiation of the letter of intent. Once the parties are paying legal fees for lease preparation and negotiation, it is too late.

Special Issues

Many single-tenant industrial/warehouse leases are written on a "triple net" basis, under which the tenant pays all taxes, insurance, and maintenance. Taxes, insurance, and maintenance may be billed to and paid directly by the tenant, or they may be paid by the landlord and reimbursed by the tenant, but in either case, the tenant is paying them in full. If the building is new, "triple net" might even include such maintenance and replacement items as roof and structure (but often excludes defects in the original construction). If the building is not new, the landlord is frequently responsible for roof and structure. The lease might still be referred to as triple net, but actually be a qualified triple-net lease. Hence, the phrase "triple net" is a shorthand

and sometimes misleading way of describing the way the rent and other charges are dealt with in the lease. That is why it is important to avoid using the phrase without having the lease actually specify who pays what.

It should be understood that the fixed rent payable under a triple-net lease is lower than what would be charged under a gross lease or a gross lease with stops. If the landlord were asked to undertake certain costs, such as insurance, the landlord would expect the fixed rent to be increased to cover those costs, and would require the tenant to accept the risk of increases of those costs. A lease in which the landlord pays taxes, insurance, and maintenance is known as a "gross lease." To protect the landlord's cash flow from the property, the lease may provide for the tenant to pay increases in those costs to the extent those costs exceed a specified base amount, or the amount payable in a base year. That is what I referred to above as "stops." I will discuss stops and their calculation below and also on page 135.

If the tenant is proposing to lease only a part of a building, the lease may still be written as a "net lease," with taxes, insurance, and maintenance being excluded from the fixed rent, but the tenant being billed by the landlord for a share of those costs. That share is usually pro rata, but under some circumstances, it may be calculated on a different basis. For example, if Tenant A has a use that requires a disproportionate share of the parking area, it is appropriate to allocate a larger share of the cost of snow removal and other parking lot maintenance to Tenant A; otherwise other tenants would be obligated to subsidize Tenant A, which would be unfair and which they would not agree to. Likewise, Tenant B may have direct access to the parking area, whereas other tenants must pass through a common corridor to which the landlord provides janitorial services. These call for allocating the cost of cleaning the common corridor to the tenants who use that service, and not to Tenant B.

The lease for that multi-tenant warehouse building might also be written as a gross lease with stops. The stops may be given as a set number, such as taxes in excess of $4 per square foot. If that is the case, the broker for the tenant should seek to find out the actual cost (or the actual anticipated cost for the first year of the lease). Because if the actual taxes or anticipated taxes are, for example, $6 per square foot and that is the number the landlord used to calculate the base rent, the tenant is paying the extra $2 in the base rent for the first year and each year thereafter during the term as part of the excess over $4. The same issue obviously applies to the other elements of the gross rental.

Straight gross leases without stops or, as they are sometimes called, full-service leases, are occasionally used. Since the landlord incurs the risk of unanticipated increases in taxes, insurance, and maintenance, the landlord will usually seek annual increases in the base rent as a hedge against that risk, or may use full-service lease forms only for leases of short duration.

Another issue common to industrial/warehouse leases is the responsibility for environmental problems. Landlords will insist that tenants who use environmentally sensitive materials assume all responsibility for those materials. Tenants will want to know the existing environmental condition of the property to ensure that they will not be responsible for preexisting conditions. Both parties may be concerned with environmental problems caused by third parties, such as the drive-by dumper or the adjoining owner. In a net lease, the landlord may seek to place that risk on the tenant and the tenant will understandably resist that.

Finally, there is an issue that is not unique to industrial/warehouse leases—the hedge against inflation. In the 1960s, many industrial/warehouse leases for single-tenant occupancy in new buildings were written for 20-year terms (which was the term of the totally nonrecourse loans used to finance the construction of those buildings). They were truly triple-net leases, but they did not provide for any increases in the fixed rent over the term. Inflation simply was not a problem at that time. It is hard to believe, but many even had options to extend at reduced rents. The theory was that once the loan was paid off and the owner did not have to service a debt, the rent was total profit, so the landlord could decrease the net rent and the tenant could benefit from the fact that there no longer was a debt to service. Those leases did not even provide for a recapture (which will be discussed on page 72), so the leases could be assigned for a fee or subleased at a higher rent, and the profit would be earned by the tenant. Needless to say, landlords do not make that mistake anymore (they make other mistakes). Landlords, instead, realize that inflation is (usually) a fact of life, and seek to provide for increases in rent over the term. In industrial/warehouse leases, that is generally done by periodic increases in rent, either by a specified dollar amount, a percentage increase, or an increase (but usually not a decrease) tied to the cost of living, using one of the indices published by the U.S. government, usually a consumer price index, or CPI.[4] Those rent adjustments are sometimes referred to as "financial escalations." This, too, will be discussed further in numerous places below.

Office Leases
Uses
Most office leases are for general office use, such as corporate offices, law offices, accounting offices, brokerage offices, bank back-office space, and general business space. Offices located in the central business district may not include parking, especially in congested areas that are well served by public transportation. Offices located in suburbs or other outlying areas may well include parking. Another common office use is medical. Medical offices often have sinks in every examining room, and bathrooms in the space rather than in the common corridor. Depending on the equipment used, the user may require extra floor bearing capacity, extra power or insulation against radiation. Sometimes offices are used for educational purposes, which means increased traffic on the elevator (often at the same time) and possibly students who are not as careful with the common areas as one would hope. A banking operation, which is somewhere between office and retail, has its own issues, since it might have a drive-through facility and special security needs. Each of these situations (and others not presented here) involves specific issues that must be dealt with in the pre-lease negotiations.

Some office buildings offer amenities that are not customarily offered in other situations. Thus a building or group of buildings may offer a conference center, a health club, child care, indoor parking, or a food venue. These amenities might be offered as a service by the building owner, or they may be areas in the building or group of buildings that are leased to operators of that type of business. Some services may be offered gratis, to increase

---

4. For the first time in my career, we witnessed the threat of deflation during the recession of 2008. If that unfortunate condition ever occurs, I can foresee some tenants asking that the rent be tied to CPI, including reductions in CPI. It might be hard to argue against.

the leasability of premises in the building (such as assigned indoor parking spaces) or may be offered on a fee basis. In either case, a strong tenant may seek to have those amenities offered for little or no extra charge.

Many office buildings are multiuse buildings. Certainly those in the central business district are likely to have retail users in the building, even if it is just a newspaper stand. Outside the central business district, it is not unusual for a bank or a restaurant to be located in the same office building. Multiuse buildings require special consideration by the brokers, as they create special issues for tenants. Those issues include the adequacy of parking, cleanliness, security, and, importantly, a proper allocation of the operating expenses for the building among the various users.

Existing office buildings do not customarily offer zoning issues to tenants. However, some uses may require confirmation that the zoning permits those uses. A bank with a drive-through for a teller or an ATM may suggest a check into zoning and other municipal requirements. Similarly, a restaurant tenant in an office building that wants outdoor dining may require special permits and will certainly have to check local municipal regulations.

Special Issues

While the costs of taxes, insurance, and certain maintenance are imposed on tenants in industrial/warehouse leases, and also in retail and other types of leases, office leases in multi-tenant buildings usually seek to allocate to tenants not only those costs but also costs unique to those office buildings, such as operating expenses. A major cost to landlords of office buildings (except in the case of single-tenant buildings, which are more like single-tenant warehouse or retail buildings) is janitorial service. That service, usually performed at night, includes cleaning offices, cleaning and sanitizing restrooms, emptying trash, washing windows, and the like. Multi-tenant office buildings usually include a right of the landlord to pass the cost of operating expenses on to the tenants. Some of the leases are net leases, as in the multi-tenant warehouse building situation. Others are gross leases with stops. Sometimes taxes are included in operating expenses, but sometimes they are a separate item of cost, either net or with a stop. Insurance is usually included. Operating expenses will be discussed in detail below (beginning on page 139).

Another major issue in most office leases is services. Whereas a warehouse may have HVAC units on the roof that provide heating and cooling to all or part of the space, the office tenant in a multi-tenant building is usually relying on the landlord's heating and cooling equipment and distribution system to keep the space comfortable. The tenant may also be relying on the building for elevators, maintenance of common areas, utilities, parking, and, as noted above, janitorial service. The broker for the tenant should check the availability and adequacy of all the services to be provided.

If the tenant is leasing in an existing office building, the tenant will not have to be very concerned about zoning. However, if the tenant has an unusual office use, it may be wise for the brokers to make certain that there is no problem.

As in industrial/warehouse leases, landlords in office leases will be looking for financial escalations.

Retail Leases

Uses

In general, retail lease uses are to sell goods and services to the public. The user may be a general merchandise store, a grocery store, a bookstore, an upscale clothing store, a discount store—you know what stores sell what merchandise. However, retail uses may also include restaurants, salons, bars, banks, currency exchanges, income tax service providers, movie theaters, health clubs, schools, day-care facilities, and other such special uses. Each of those special uses represents a unique set of issues to be resolved in the lease and in the lease negotiations, and may also involve zoning and regulatory issues.

Special Issues

Financial escalation is a major issue in retail leases. Some leases handle financial escalation with a specified dollar amount, a percentage, or a cost-of-living adjustment (see page 121). However, in retail leasing, there is an additional way (which may be used instead of the others or in addition). That is percentage rent.

In a lease with percentage rent, the tenant is obligated to pay a certain percentage of its gross sales, usually above a specified amount, or "break point." The break point may be an agreed sum, unrelated to fixed minimum rent, or an amount calculated by dividing the amount of fixed minimum rent by a percentage to determine the "natural break point." For an example of a natural break point, assume the fixed minimum rent is $80,000 per year and the percentage is 6 percent. In that case, the break point will be calculated by dividing $80,000 by .06, the answer being $1,333,333.33. Another way of looking at this is that the rent is always 6 percent of gross sales, but if gross sales do not reach the natural break point, the tenant still pays a fixed minimum amount. The lease might provide more than one break point. To do so, it would specify one break point and its related percentage, and then provide for a second or even a third break point and different percentages if gross sales exceed the amounts specified. The percentages over the additional break points may be more or less dependent on the nature of the use or simply based on the deal negotiated by the parties. Thus, the lease may provide for percentage rent equal to 5 percent of gross sales in excess of $1 million and up to $2 million, 4 percent of gross in excess of $2 million and up to $3 million, and 3 percent of gross sales in excess of $3 million.

There are other issues related to percentage rent. First, the lease must define "gross sales." Second, it must provide for some method for record retention by the tenant and for the landlord to have the right to audit the tenant's records to confirm that the correct amount of gross sales have been reported and the correct amount of percentage rent has been paid. Third, the landlord will generally require the tenant to agree not to compete within a specified radius of the location of the leased premises. Obviously, the third item is to prevent the tenant from opening a competing business nearby and diverting sales from the leased premises to the other location. The specified radius is usually referred to as the "trading area."[5] Percentage rent issues will be further discussed below (see page 129).

It is not unusual for a tenant in a shopping center to request the exclusive right to sell its type of products on that property (and possibly other property owned by the landlord that is nearby). The obvious purpose is to

---

5. Sometimes a lease might include a trading area even in the absence of percentage rent if the landlord is relying on a particular store to generate business in its shopping center.

prevent competition with the tenant's business. Exclusives create serious problems for landlords. First, agreeing to an exclusive might be an antitrust violation. In addition, the requested exclusive use might be too broad. For example, a tenant that sells cosmetics might ask for an exclusive regarding the sale of cosmetics. If the landlord agrees to that broad exclusive, it has eliminated the possibility of leasing to a drugstore or a department store, both of which sell cosmetics, but not as their primary use. The landlord may negotiate for an exclusion for those specific stores, but more likely the landlord will limit the exclusive to the sale of cosmetics as the primary use of the other tenant. In addition, the tenant may request a provision that states that the sale of the item by another in violation of the exclusive is a default by the landlord. This requires the landlord to police other tenants' operations, and possibly having to terminate another lease for violation of the exclusive. Landlords do not want to be put in the position of having to sue another tenant or being in default under the lease with the tenant having the exclusive. The way that is usually handled is to provide that the landlord "will not lease to another tenant whose primary use is [the excluded use]." If the lease contains such a provision and the landlord does not lease for that purpose, but another tenant sells the prohibited goods, the landlord may require the other tenant to stop doing so as a violation of its permitted-use clause, or the lease with the first tenant may permit the first tenant to sue to prevent the violation of the exclusive. Obviously, the broker for the tenant who is seeking the exclusive will want the broadest language in the exclusive in order to eliminate the competitive use and to require the landlord to be involved in enforcing it. The landlord's broker will resist that.

Specialty retail leases (i.e., other than retail sale of merchandise) present other issues. A restaurant will create odors, invite vermin, have garbage storage and pickup issues, or be open extended hours. If it is a restaurant serving food for off-premises consumption, it may create debris in a shopping center or on the adjoining street. A restaurant or bar serving liquor will have to have a liquor license and may have to carry "dramshop" insurance if there is liability imposed on sellers of alcoholic beverages to people who have already had enough to drink. The restaurant or bar will also have later hours than the rest of the center, which creates additional issues for the shopping center landlord. Some jurisdictions prohibit the sale of liquor within a certain distance of a school or church. Specialty retail leases may require variances or special-use permits to comply with zoning. One use that leaps to mind is auto (especially used car) sales, which may be specifically addressed in the zoning ordinance.

A bank has special security issues. If the landlord is providing janitorial services, such as in a mixed-use building, the bank will probably want its own people to perform that function, which will affect the operating expense calculation, not only for the bank, but also for the remaining tenants who are served by the janitorial service. A movie theater has special parking requirements and extended hours. It might contain a restaurant and will certainly sell refreshments, which creates problems similar to those of restaurants. Suffice it to say that movie theater leases offer many complications. A health club may require extra floor support for its heavy equipment, and it may generate a lot of noise. A day-care center has numerous requirements to comply with licensing laws and protection of the children and may also create a noise issue, especially if the children have an outdoor play area.

In mixed-use buildings, the method of allocating taxes, operating expenses or common-area expenses is quite complicated, and the parties may have differing ideas as to what is a fair allocation. There are also issues of access and security that may have to be dealt with.

Ground Leases
Uses

Ground leases are often used when, for some reason, the owner of the property cannot or does not want to sell it, but wants some of the benefits from the real estate; or the prospective tenant cannot raise the equity to buy the land for its intended use, but is able to fund the construction of new improvements on the property; or the landlord wants its property developed and does not have the capital or know-how to do so. The ground lease is thus a form of financing.

Ground leases are much more common in some parts of the country than in others. They are more prevalent in New York, for example, than in the Midwest. They are very useful if the property is appropriate for development or redevelopment. For example, a piece of land may have had an obsolete strip mall on it and be suitable, physically and economically, for a mid-rise office building. The tenant will seek a lease long enough to use up the useful life of the improvement and to obtain the financing to demolish the old structure and construct the new one. Needless to say, the tenant may not undertake to sign a ground lease and construct a building without a firm commitment for a lease or leases (unless it proposes to use the property for its own business). A lease will be a requirement for the tenant to finance the project. Thus the ground lease will likely be for a minimum term of 40 years, and perhaps for as long as 99 years, either as the primary term or the primary term with options to extend.

Another form of ground lease occurs when a landlord simply leases a vacant lot to a tenant for use as a parking lot or for storage. That situation is more analogous to an industrial/warehouse lease and will not be further considered here.

Special Issues

Since ground leases are, in a sense, a sale of vacant land (since the term is so long and the tenant intends to build new improvements on the property), the tenant will have to approach the leasing as it would a purchase. It will have to have a due diligence period to determine the suitability of the property for the intended use. It may even make the deal contingent on the execution of a sublease or subleases for proposed building. Thus, if the tenant is entering into the ground lease because it is negotiating a build-and-lease deal with, for example, a movie theater, it will want the right to terminate the ground lease if it fails to reach agreement with the prospective theater tenant.

Needless to say, whether the ground lease involves property with existing improvements or vacant property, if the use is to be changed, the brokers will be concerned with zoning and will have to confirm that its proposed use and structure will comply.

In addition, the tenant is concerned about protecting its subtenants in the event that the ground lease is terminated for any reason. It will want the lease to provide that the landlord will not terminate non-defaulting subtenants if the ground tenant, as the prime tenant, defaults and the ground lease itself is terminated. It is in the landlord's interest to agree to that because the subtenants will, in all probability, be obligated to pay a much higher rent than the ground tenant, who will have built the building to house the subtenants under the ground lease.

The landlord has special concerns, as well. Inasmuch as a default by the tenant will, unless the tenant's mortgagee takes over the lease, put the landlord in possession of the improved property (probably subject to the subleases the tenant has made), the landlord will want some input, or at least approval rights, as to the improvements the tenant intends to construct on its land.

Since it is feasible for the tenant to obtain financing secured by its lease by means of a leasehold mortgage or a leasehold deed of trust, the tenant will need language in the ground lease that protects its lender against the lease being terminated if it defaults under the ground lease. These protections are quite extensive, including rights and time to cure, and the right to a new lease if the ground lease is terminated, either because of the default or because of the bankruptcy of the tenant. The ground lease must have a sufficiently long term (including tenant options to extend) so that there is value in the remaining term for the lender, and the lender will want liberal rights to assign the lease if it finds a buyer for it.

Sometimes the lender under leasehold financing seeks to require that the ground landlord mortgage its fee interest in the property to secure its mortgage. Unless there is some special benefit to the landlord, it is certainly not in the interest of the landlord to place its interest in the property at risk to secure a loan to its tenant.

An additional landlord concern is the amount of the rent. I once represented a tenant at the end of a ground lease in downtown Chicago of 99 years in which the rent (payable in gold) was not increased during the term and in which the tenant had a right to a "new lease" for an additional term of 40 years at the end of the 99 years, at an increased but fixed rent. Apparently no one in 1879 considered that there might be inflation. Today we are more sensitive to the risk of inflation and build financial escalations into our ground leases.

Everyone "knows" that even if a lease provides for payment in gold, the rent cannot actually be collected in gold, right? Well, that is only partially true. Provided that the ground lease was in existence in 1933, when it became illegal to require payment in gold, the landlord cannot enforce that provision. However, for contracts made after October 1977, gold payment is legal. Let's say someone takes an assignment today of the tenant's interest in an old ground lease (and there are still many 99-year leases in effect) and the effect of the assignment is to terminate the liability of the old tenant under the lease. The assignment will constitute what we lawyers call a "novation." In plain language, it is considered a new lease.[6] Whoops, the requirement for payment in gold is reinstated. When the lease was made in 1925, or thereabouts, the official United State price for gold was $20.67 per troy ounce.[7] At this time, gold prices fluctuate constantly, but are generally well over $1,000 per troy ounce. So how much more would it cost to buy an equivalent amount of gold to pay the equivalent number of gold coins specified in the lease? I had a deal in which I was representing the assignee. It was pure luck that I recalled hearing about a change in the law (it was just a comment I heard in passing and I was not confronting the issue at the time). Because of that, we structured the deal as a sublease (without the old tenant being released) and the deal went forward without the risk. It is a trap for the unwary, and if it is all you remember from reading this book, it may stand you in good stead, since an assignee's attorney or the broker may not be aware of the 1977 law but the landlord's lawyer or its broker may be.

Because the landlord's value in the lease is in the building, it is customarily provided that once the building is completed, the tenant no longer has personal liability for the performance of the obligations. This is an additional reason the landlord wants input as to the improvements and possibly as to the subtenants. It should be noted that this makes the ground leases pretty freely assignable. That raises a very interesting issue, and one that brokers should be aware of, since an assignment could cost the assignee a great deal of money, or the tenant/assignor could make a considerable profit.

An important issue to be considered is what happens to the buildings at the end of the term. Generally, the ground lease will provide that the

---

6. If you are concerned with this, see 216 Jamaican Avenue, LLC v. S&R Playhouse Realty Co., 540 F.3d 433 (6th Cir. 2008).

7. See www.nma.org/pdf/gold/his_gold_prices.pdf.

improvements are deemed to be real estate belonging to the tenant (so the tenant may take advantage of depreciation and other benefits of owner-ship) and that they become the property of the landlord at the end of the term of the ground lease. But does the landlord want them? A building built early in the term of the 99-year lease, or even a 40-year lease, may be totally obsolete and require demolition. Who is to pay for that? On the other hand, what if somewhere in the middle of a 40-year ground lease, the tenant demolishes the improvements and erects new, state-of-the art facilities? Perhaps the landlord may want that. Maybe the tenant, with the landlord's consent, has entered into a sublease extending beyond the expi-ration of the term of the ground lease. Certainly the improvements should not be demolished under those circumstances. Even though the original negotiators of the ground lease may no longer be around when it expires, they must project themselves into the unknown future so that their clients or the clients' successors are not trapped by those problems that they can, at least, anticipate to occur at the end of the ground lease term.

Government Leases

Government leases are a special animal. I had a client who avoided them like the plague. Another client owned office buildings in a state capital and government leases were his bread and butter.

There are actually some advantages to landlords in government leases, particularly federal government leases, in which collecting rent is assured. The major advantage is that governments need a lot of space and they need it in good times and bad. The main disadvantage of government leases is that the landlord is subject to the annual appropriation process, and the lease may be terminated if no money is appropriated for the agency or for a particular lease. If the government entity is short of money, as most are, one of two things might happen. First, the government may delay paying its bills, including rents. This presents serious problems with lenders, as you can well understand. Second, the government may downsize its operations and terminate the lease. Getting a governmental entity to lease a particular space may be a problem because of political pressure to lease another space, even if it is less suitable for the entity's needs. And corruption might get in the way of a deal, or may cause a deal to be made, giving rise to adverse publicity or even criminal prosecution of the landlord.

Rent on government leases is typically paid in arrears, which should not be much of a problem if the rent is actually paid in arrears, but on time. The landlord may have to front the first month's mortgage payment, but that should not be a major deterrent. More serious problems are that government leases are usually signed on the government's form and governments are not particularly eager to negotiate changes. Also, many government agencies are poor housekeepers. When the landlord gets the space back, it may need a lot of fix-up, especially if the agency has a lot of people serviced by it. For example, a social security office or an unemployment office has a lot of users who may not be too sensitive to the need to help maintain the condition of the premises.

With all the disadvantages, I suppose government leases are better than no leases, so they keep being made. It is just wise to be aware of the problems.

Subleases

Subleases present a dilemma. Subleasing is much more complicated than direct leasing, but pressure exists to create a simple and inexpensive sublease document. A regular lease basically deals with the rights and obligations of only two parties, the landlord and the tenant. In a sublease, the rights and obligations established in the prime lease between the prime landlord and the prime tenant (being the sublandlord) have a substantial and often controlling effect on the deal between the sublandlord and the subtenant. The sublease situation is further complicated by the fact that there is no direct relationship between the prime landlord and the subtenant and because the subtenant's use is often different from the sublandlord's. Despite these inherent complications, the parties to a sublease seek that simple document for many reasons. Principally, they may think that because the terms of the lease have already been negotiated between the prime landlord and the sublandlord, the parties to the sublease should not have to revisit settled issues. Additionally, the parties may not understand the complexity of the sublease situation. They may think that it should be a simple matter to transfer the terms pertaining to the occupancy of the premises from the prime lease to a sublease. Especially in sublease situations for a short term, a small area, or both, the parties do not see a justification for dealing at length (and expensively) with complications, particularly if they do not perceive that the complications exist.

Three traditional approaches to the drafting of subleases exist. I call the first the full sublease or the "all-inclusive" approach, the second the "incorporation by reference" approach, and the third the "haphazard" approach.

In the all-inclusive approach, the drafter creates an entirely new lease between the sublandlord and the subtenant, using the prime lease as a point of reference. This new lease may track the form of the prime lease, but will allocate among the prime landlord, the sublandlord, and the subtenant all of the benefits and burdens in the prime lease. At some other place in the sublease, the parties may create a mechanism for the enforcement for the subtenant of the prime landlord's obligations. Because no direct relationship exists between the prime landlord and the subtenant, enforcement against the prime landlord will have to be pursued, if at all, by the sublandlord on the subtenant's behalf, and the sublease may include a provision requiring the sublandlord to enforce the provisions of the prime lease for the benefit of the subtenant, usually at the subtenant's expense. The all-inclusive sublease may also be on a completely new form that, apart from its references to the prime lease, does not resemble or track the prime lease at all. While perhaps dealing thoroughly with the issues, this approach will often unnecessarily prolong and complicate negotiations because, in addition to the drafting time required to create the instrument, the form itself may encourage negotiation of provisions that already have been dealt with in the prime lease and may not be meaningfully altered. I have done such a lease only once in my career.

In the incorporation-by-reference approach, the drafter sets forth the agreements that apply between the sublandlord and the subtenant only; those agreements are the business terms of the sublease. The drafter then incorporates by reference certain sections of the prime lease that are to apply between the sublandlord and the subtenant. The drafter usually states that the references in the prime lease to the "landlord" shall be deemed to be references to the "sublandlord," and likewise that the references in the prime lease to the "tenant" shall be deemed to be references to the "subtenant." The better-drafted incorporation-by-reference subleases will qualify those obligations of the prime landlord that are to remain with the prime landlord and those that are to be performed by, or for the benefit of, the sublandlord. As in the all-inclusive approach, some provision is usually made for the enforcement of the obligations of the prime landlord for the benefit of the subtenant. The incorporation-by-reference approach is the one most frequently used, but it is not terribly efficient because the parties have to be certain that the appropriate provisions in the prime lease are incorporated or excluded from the incorporation.

In the haphazard approach, the drafter may pull a lease form from the shelf, name it a "sublease," change the references to identify the parties as "sublandlord" and "subtenant," and use the phrase "hereby subleases" instead of "hereby leases." This type of sublease may have a section prohibiting each party from causing a default under the prime lease, but it does not meaningfully allocate the rights and obligations of the three parties.

Both the all-inclusive approach and the incorporation-by-reference approach have advantages and disadvantages. The haphazard approach has no advantages.

With my friend and colleague, Marty Miner, a partner with the law firm of Holland & Knight in New York, I considered this situation and we proposed an alternative approach: a generic sublease. In a sense, the creation of a generic sublease attempts to accomplish the impossible. It seeks to create a vehicle that will serve in all situations, whether office, industrial/warehouse, retail, or even residential. It also seeks to coexist with any prime lease no matter what the covenants and agreements between the prime landlord and the sublandlord may be. The proposed form attempts to accomplish this by dealing first with the business terms of the sublease transaction and the other agreements that apply solely between the sublandlord and the subtenant, and then dealing with issues that are unique to the sublease situation. The business terms and the agreements that apply between the sublandlord and subtenant are typical of any lease situation and do not require further discussion. However, the way that the form deals with the sublease issues does require attention. First, the sublease identifies the prime lease but does not directly incorporate it by reference. Second, the sublease seeks to allocate responsibilities that are the sublandlord's under the prime lease but that are undertaken, in whole or in part, by the subtenant under the sublease.

Third, the sublease seeks to prevent the subtenant from doing things not permitted without the prime landlord's consent unless such consent (as well as that of the sublandlord) is obtained. Fourth, it contains a set of provisions that deal directly with a number of the issues that are created in the sublease situation. Finally, it contains provisions that are often inserted in a prime landlord's consent to the sublease.

As to this final point, it should be noted that prime landlords are not particularly shy about seeking benefits when they are asked to consent to a sublease. For example, they might ask for additional security deposits or for other amendments to the prime lease or even the sublease itself, and those requests might affect either the sublandlord, the subtenant, or both. If the prime lease provides that consent may not be unreasonably withheld, such conditions to a consent may not really be permissible, but very few tenants have the time, the money, or the inclination to litigate over the matter.[8] Three-party discussions may be required to resolve those issues, and it is really impossible to prevent that situation when negotiating the sublease, or even at the time the prime lease is entered into.

It is not my purpose to include any forms in this book. If, however, you want to get a sublease done efficiently, you may refer the drafting lawyer to the article "Subleases: A New Approach Revisited," in *Real Property, Trust and Estate Law Journal* (Spring 2006), or to an earlier version of the sublease (and a longer explanation) in the article, "Subleases: A New Approach-A Proposal," *Real Property, Trust and Estate Law Journal* (Spring 1999). Of course, those forms, like any forms, will have to be modified when used in order to fit the particulars of the pending deal.

---

8. Some leases provide that consent will not be unreasonably withheld, conditioned, or delayed. That is fine, but if a consent is unreasonably conditioned or delayed unreasonably, is it not also being unreasonably withheld?

PART II

LEASE PROVISIONS COMMON TO MOST LEASES

I admit that I approach this section with some trepidation. I have read lease provision analyses, and they are usually as dry as dust. I hope that is not my style of writing. I shall do my best to make this section as readable as the prior ones so that the information presented is not just reference material, but an enjoyable read. Here is how I propose to handle this material: First I shall discuss, in no particular order, a number of provisions common to most types of leases. Then, when I have sufficiently whetted your appetite, I will delve into provisions that are specific to certain types of leases. Here goes!

Subordination and Non-Disturbance

Subordination and non-disturbance may seem a strange provision to start with, but remember the poor broker who did a restaurant lease without the benefit of a lawyer? (See page 11.) Recall that he had to pay through the nose because of some "legal mumbo jumbo." Well, I am going to help you understand what that mumbo jumbo is about so you can contribute to the protection of your tenant client. It is really pretty understandable. Just remember the phrase, "first in time, first in right."

We are dealing here with the question of which has priority—the lease or the mortgage.[1] If a mortgage is executed, delivered, and recorded before

---

1. In many states, the borrower delivers a "trust deed" or "deed of trust" to the lender or to a third party in trust for the lender. There are some technical reasons for that under applicable state law that are not necessary to discuss here. The trust deed or deed of trust has the effect of a mortgage for the purpose under discussion, and in this book I refer to "mortgage" for convenience.

41

a lease is executed and delivered, the lender has priority over the lease; if it forecloses, it can wipe the lease out.[2] If the lease is executed and delivered before the mortgage is, and the mortgagee has notice (by recording of a memorandum of lease) or actual knowledge of the existence of the lease (such as by inspecting the property and seeing the tenant building out the space or conducting its business), the lease has priority; if there is a foreclosure, the lender cannot wipe out the lease. So far so good?

What happens if your tenant is about to sign a lease in which it will be spending a lot of money to fix the place up, or the lease is for a long term and/or for a lot of space, and there is already a mortgage in place? How do you protect your tenant? You make certain that the tenant gets a non-disturbance agreement, that's how! "What is a non-disturbance agreement?" you ask. It is an agreement by the lender with the priority position that, if there is a foreclosure, neither it, nor another party that buys at the foreclosure sale, will evict that tenant.[3]

A simple agreement not to evict—the "non-disturbance" aspect of the agreement—is fine, but it certainly does not go far enough. The tenant must also be concerned about who will perform the obligations of the landlord under the lease after the foreclosure. Who will arrange to have the offices cleaned, or maintain the roof and structure, or remove snow and ice from the parking lot, if those undertakings by the landlord are included in the lease. The tenant needs an undertaking in the agreement by the lender to do those things. It is sometimes referred to in the agreement as "recognition," or there is simply an agreement to perform the obligations. That agreement is not open ended, however. Lenders will, typically, not agree to return a security deposit if they have not actually received it from the landlord, or to cure landlord defaults that occurred before the lender takes over the property (except, possibly, a continuing default), or to be bound by payments of rent more than one month in advance (if the rent is payable monthly),

---

2. Recording is not generally a condition if the tenant has actual knowledge of the existence of the mortgage, but mortgages are almost universally recorded.

3. The same principle applies if the landlord is actually a tenant under a ground lease. If the ground lease exists prior to your tenant's lease, that ground lessor would have the right to terminate the ground lease if its lessee (your landlord) defaults, which would, in the absence of a non-disturbance agreement, cause the eviction of the tenant.

or to be bound by a tenant right to set off any amounts due to the tenant because of a default by the original landlord against future payments of rent. The lender will also require that the tenant attorn to the lender if the lender becomes the successor landlord by reason of the foreclosure. "Attorn" simply means that the tenant becomes bound to perform its obligations for the benefit of the lender, just as the lender has agreed to become bound to perform obligations for the tenant's benefit. The provisions of a non-disturbance agreement may be negotiable to some extent. For example, if the landlord has agreed to a tenant allowance, the lender may agree to allow the tenant to set off any unpaid allowance against rent payable after the foreclosure. This is extremely important in leases where a tenant is to receive a substantial payment to help pay for tenant improvements. Otherwise the payment right might be lost in the foreclosure.

Sometimes the lease itself provides that the tenant will not be disturbed and will be entitled to recognition in the event of a foreclosure. That provision is useless to the tenant. The agreement must come from the lender who then has a mortgage on the property. The agreement should also be recorded in order to protect the tenant if the mortgage is assigned by the lender or if someone other than the lender buys the property at the foreclosure sale (or subsequently from the lender itself). If a non-disturbance agreement cannot be signed simultaneously with the execution of the lease, then a tenant who needs the protection should reserve the right to terminate the lease if the agreement is not concluded within a specified period.

If the lease has priority over a new mortgage, the lender might ask the tenant to subordinate its prior position to the lender. Many lease forms provide that the tenant will subordinate its positions to a new mortgagee, but do not condition the tenant's obligation to do so on the mortgagee's agreeing to recognition and non-disturbance. That is unfair to the tenant; why should the tenant be required to give up a right it already has by being first in time without adequate protection? In my judgment, even small tenants should negotiate that protection. That is the fair result. The lease should be revised to provide that if the lender requires subordination, it will be obligated to provide non-disturbance and recognition, as described above, as part of the subordination agreement.

My discussion of subordination and non-disturbance highlights a basic principle in lease review that cannot be emphasized enough: *every provision in a lease has an economic effect.* It is there to provide some benefit or protection, or cost or risk, to the parties. Every provision, even the most mundane or obscure, must be carefully considered. *There are no "boilerplate" provisions in a lease.*

The Parties

Landlord

Who is the landlord, anyway? You, as the tenant rep broker, should ask yourself: Is it some entity that could possibly default in its mortgage and thus put my tenant client in trouble? Will my tenant actually collect the promised allowance for tenant improvements? Does the landlord named in the lease really own the property? And most importantly: How do I even know if I will collect a commission?

The answer to those questions is important, but chances are you will not really find out the identity of the principals of the landlord. The landlord will be an entity, such as a limited liability company, created to limit the owners' exposure. If that entity is member managed, you will be able to find out the members, but if it is manager managed, you will only find out the manager, which may, in turn, be another entity. Even if the property is owned by an individual or a family, the title may still be in a limited liability company, and it may be manager managed.

As to the landlord's ownership of the property, that is not a common risk, but the only sure way for a tenant to protect itself is to obtain leasehold title insurance (see page 93). However, that insurance is most typically obtained in situations where an entire property is being leased (as in a ground lease) or the lease is for a major space.

I cannot answer the commission issue. You may be able to satisfy yourself by questioning the landlord's broker or by talking to whoever is negotiating on behalf of the landlord. It is the payment of the tenant allowance or other concessions that is the serious issue for the tenant. The payment might be coming out of loan proceeds, but there are two risks there. First, the lender might not be solvent. Second, the landlord might default and give the lender a basis not to fund the allowance. There are a couple of ways the tenant can protect itself. It can insist on a right of set-off against rent if the allowance is not paid. That is not a perfect solution, because it means that the tenant will have to advance the payment for the improvements (which it may not be able to finance) and only later get it back by savings in rent payments. Or it might ask the landlord to provide security for the payment, preferably in the form of a letter of credit from a substantial bank.

Tenant

Similar questions and issues arise in connection with the identity of the tenant. Is the landlord getting an entity that actually exists? Is it a separate entity or a division of another entity? Does the financial data provided give an accurate description of the financial position of the entity that is to be the tenant?

Let us assume that the proposed tenant is a major company known as ABC, Inc., that you represent the landlord, and a tenant rep broker proposes a lease in which the tenant is not ABC, Inc., but is ABC Company. First, you as landlord, broker, or the lawyer for the landlord, can look up the records of the secretary of state where the tenant is said to be incorporated (or organized, if it is a limited liability company). You may find that it is listed, but if you do not find it, you may be advised that it is really a "division" of ABC, Inc. A division of an entity is not a separate entity and does not ordinarily have the legal authority to sign leases or other contracts. The tenant should really be ABC, Inc., but you are told that the authorized officers of ABC, Inc. do not sign division leases for premises of this size. Next, you ask for a corporate resolution from ABC, Inc.'s board of directors authorizing the division officers to sign the lease and you are told that none exists, but at the next meeting in three weeks, one may be passed, but probably will not be. You and more importantly, your client, want the lease and are "assured" that there will be no problem, that other landlords have signed leases with this "entity." In fact, you are the only one who has ever questioned it (this is to try to make you feel bad or foolish, but you should really feel proud that you have raised a real and material issue). Once the tenant moves in, it cannot say that it was not authorized, because there will have been substantial part performance by the tenant in accepting delivery of the space by the landlord and substantial part performance binds the tenant even if the person signing the lease was not authorized to do so. On the other hand, it could be a major problem if the landlord is being called upon to do substantial build-out, which will take considerable time, during which the tenant may say that the division was not authorized to sign the lease, that its acts were what we lawyers call "ultra vires," or beyond the signer's power, and therefore not binding. I have no easy answer for this one. It becomes the landlord's business call.

Let's change the facts a little. Let us assume that ABC Company is not a division of ABC, Inc., but its subsidiary. A subsidiary is a separate entity and has authority to sign leases. Good! The landlord asks for a financial statement and is promptly sent an annual report—of ABC, Inc. Where is the financial statement of ABC Company? There is none. ABC, Inc.'s annual report, which contains its current financial statements, is a consolidated statement of ABC, Inc., its subsidiaries, and divisions. There is no statement for ABC Company, even though that is the tenant, not ABC, Inc. Does ABC Company have the wherewithal to perform its obligations under the lease? You do not know. You may request whatever financial data is available for ABC Company, but it may be pretty sketchy. Will ABC, Inc. guarantee the obligations under the lease? Maybe it will or maybe it won't. Will ABC Company put up a substantial security deposit? Maybe it will or maybe it won't. Another business call.

All right, you have convinced ABC, Inc. to sign the lease for ABC Company as its division. You receive the lease and it is signed by the division president. That is another problem. What authority does the division president have to bind ABC, Inc. to the lease, even one for that division? Only the president of a corporation (not a division president) or the manager of a limited liability company, has *apparent* authority to sign leases or other contracts. You ask for a corporate resolution but get the same answer as before—none exists and none is likely to exist. Business call again.

Insurance

Insurance is kind of a wilderness for many brokers, and even for many lawyers. A lot of us simply do not know enough about it, so we pass the responsibility for the review of the language to insurance agents or risk managers. While it is a good idea for a broker representing a landlord to have a knowledgeable insurance person review the language when it is drafted into the lease form, it does not often happen. That is why many leases still refer to "comprehensive liability insurance" when the real name, other than for automobile insurance, is "commercial liability insurance," or why leases have low insurance amounts or have different amounts for personal injury and for property damage, when policies are now written with a combined single limit, or why leases still refer to the National Board of Underwriters, which has not existed since the 1930s.

The following is a primer on the treatment of insurable risks in commercial leases. Although it is rather long, I hope you find it useful.

It is also a good idea for the broker representing the tenant to have its insurance person review the insurance-related provisions to confirm that the tenant has or will be able to get the required coverage. It should be noted that there are more sections in the lease that are insurance affected than the ones labeled "insurance." Those include the sections pertaining to waiver of claims, waiver of the right of subrogation, indemnities, and fire and casualty, all of which are discussed below.

Simply stated, leases must deal with three insurance issues:

- Who causes what loss to whom or to whose property?
- Who has the ultimate liability for the loss?
- Whose insurance is going to pay for it?

Every landlord's lease form deals with those issues and every tenant wishes to minimize its own risk.

Liability arises when one party injures another or damages the other's property, usually as a result of some sort of fault such as negligence or deliberate misconduct. Liability is imposed to compensate the victim for the loss or damage occasioned by that wrongful act. The most common form of liability arises out of automobile accidents, but the real estate professional is aware that the issue often arises when a person slips and falls on real estate or when personal property is damaged as a result of such things as falling ceiling tiles or leaking roofs.

A property loss occurs as a result of a casualty that causes the damage or destruction of property, real or personal. A common type of such a casualty is fire, but damage caused by high winds or other natural occurrences is also a casualty loss.

Businesses purchase property insurance to create a source of funds from which to recover for property damage resulting from a casualty;[4] they also carry separate liability insurance (frequently with different insurance companies) to provide a defense and funds that they can use to pay third parties for losses that they caused. Although they tend to think that these two sorts of risks are not interrelated, the loss arising from a casualty that is caused by the negligence or other fault of one party and causes a loss to a second party may be insured both by the liability coverage of the party at fault and by the property insurance of the injured party. For example, assume that a building owner is inspecting the roof and drops a cigarette, causing a fire that damages the tenant's merchandise or machinery and equipment. The loss is covered by the building owner's liability insurance, but might also be covered by the tenant's contents insurance, which is a form of property insurance. Conversely, if the tenant's employee throws a lighted match in a wastebasket and causes the building to be substantially damaged by fire, the damage is covered by the landlord's property insurance on the building and may also be covered by the tenant's liability insurance.

If both parties carry property insurance and liability insurance, why is it necessary for the lease to deal with insurance issues at all? Or why should the lease not provide that the party at fault bear the loss and, to the extent that the loss is not covered by liability insurance, the property insurance of the other party pay the balance? The relevant provisions of many leases deal with the risks in just this way, but this arrangement is not the most economical way to deal with those risks, nor is it necessarily in the best interest of either party.

---

4. Insurance professionals and real estate professionals have a nomenclature problem. Real estate professionals tend to refer to risks involving "fire and other casualty" as "casualty" risks and refer to "property damage" as a liability issue (as in "personal injury and property damage"). Insurance professionals use the word "casualty" to refer to an occurrence causing damage and define insurance covering "fire or other casualty" as "property insurance." I will use the insurance companies' terminology, referring to "property insurance," "liability insurance," and, where appropriate, "property damage liability insurance."

The basic problem relates to limits on the proceeds of insurance policies. Property insurance typically is tied in some way to the value of the property, whereas liability insurance is purchased with a somewhat arbitrarily determined maximum level. Until several years ago, it was typical to carry liability insurance for damage to property in an amount of only between $250,000 and $500,000 per occurrence. Today, the insured customarily obtains a personal injury and property damage liability policy with a combined single limit of, for example, $3 million. Substantial excess liability (or "umbrella") coverage with higher limits may also be purchased.

Thus, if the tenant's employee (in the second example) caused a building with a replacement cost of $50 million to be totally destroyed, the landlord's property insurance, if purchased with at least that insurance limit, would probably pay the entire loss. But the parties would discover that if the tenant's property damage liability insurance were applied to the loss, the maximum amount of recovery is the policy limit, which probably is substantially less than $50 million. Similarly, the destruction of extremely valuable machinery and equipment (computer equipment or very costly merchandise) as a result of the landlord's negligence might not be adequately covered by the landlord's property damage liability insurance.

A further complication is the fact that, under common law, any person causing damage by his negligence or other wrongful act has liability for the damage, whether or not he has liability insurance to cover that loss. Thus, in the example in which the tenant's employee caused the building to burn down, the landlord has the right to sue the tenant (the tenant is liable for the negligent act of its employee performed in the course of his or her employment), whether or not the tenant has liability insurance and whether or not that insurance provides coverage or is adequate.

In fact, if the landlord's property insurance carrier pays the landlord for the loss of the building, the insurance carrier has the right under common law to sue the tenant (the party at fault) to recover the amount that it paid to the landlord. The right of the insurance company to stand in the shoes of its insured and to bring the insured's negligence claim against the party at fault is called a "right of subrogation."[5] Whether the lawsuit is brought by

---

5. "Subrogation" and "subordination" may sound the same, but they are different and

the landlord or the landlord's insurance company, it could result in liability imposed upon the tenant for an amount far in excess of the tenant's liability insurance coverage. Obviously, the same principles apply in the example in which the landlord's negligence caused the extensive loss to the tenant.

You can see that it is in the interest of all parties to have losses arising out of the damage or destruction of their property paid by a property insurance carrier and somehow to negate both the right to action of the party owning the damaged property and the right of subrogation of that party's property insurance carrier. Both of these ends can, with some limitations, be accomplished in the lease. I recommend the following three-pronged approach.

Each party should be required to carry property insurance with appropriate coverage and appropriate amounts (see the following discussion); each party should waive its right to claims for damage to its property arising out of the negligence or wrongful act of the other party; each party should agree to obtain from its insurance carrier a waiver of the right of subrogation. The waiver of subrogation might, in fact, be evidenced by a provision in the insurance policy that the coverage is not invalidated by reason of the fact that the insured has, prior to a loss, waived its right to proceed against a party at fault causing the damage or destruction of the property insured by the policy.

These three requirements—insurance coverage, waiver of claims, and waiver of subrogation rights—go a long way toward eliminating fault as the basis for paying for damage or destruction of property and limit coverage of that risk to the property insurance of the party owning the property.

Waiver of Claims and Waiver of Subrogation

Many leases contain specific provisions to the effect that the tenant waives claims against the landlord for property damage. It is not as common that there are such specific provisions for the benefit of the tenant. On the other hand, most (but not all) waivers of subrogation provisions are mutual and protect each party. A mutual waiver of subrogation provision, to be effective, should also contain a waiver of claims and provide for a waiver of subrogation so long as such protection is available from insurance carriers, plus provisions for notice if such a benefit is either not available or available only at additional cost. The right of the insured to waive (prior to a loss)

---

unrelated. Do not become confused.

the right of subrogation is now common in the insurance industry. As a rule, insurance companies make such waivers generally available because their premiums are based on risk factors that do not include an anticipation of recovery of the proceeds of the insurance from a third party. In other words, property insurers do not think they will be able to recover from third parties (whose identity may not even be known), so they calculate the insured's premium on the assumption that no such recovery will be possible.

Sometimes language drafted into the lease is evenhanded and is generally acceptable to both landlords and tenants. However, some waiver of claims provisions and mutual waiver of subrogation provisions contain unacceptable and dangerous language because they deal with matters other than property damage or they do not sufficiently eliminate fault from the allocation of risk. For example, waivers of claims provisions frequently refer to "injury to persons." They are asking the tenant to waive claims for personal injury, as well as property damage, even though personal injury is not a risk compensated by the tenant's property insurance. This is unfair to injured people because it may deprive them of the right to recover damages. Tenants should reject a waiver of claims for personal injury in a lease.[6] Many jurisdictions have statutes or case law that state that such waivers of claims of personal injury are void as against public policy.

Some waivers of subrogation are, unfortunately, not *mutual* waivers. Sometimes landlord-prepared forms require the tenant to waive claims against the landlord, and they require the tenant's insurance carrier to waive its right of subrogation against the landlord; however, they contain no reciprocal landlord agreements for the benefit of the tenant. Some waivers of subrogation provide that the waiver applies only to the extent of *collectible* insurance proceeds. This is a substantial limit on the benefits of the waiver if the party that owns the damaged property has no property insurance or has inadequate property insurance (or if it gave the insurance carrier a defense against the payment of insurance proceeds, for example, by making false statements when it procured the insurance).

---

6. If the tenant is an entity, the waiver by that entity does not bind the employees of that entity who are injured. Even if the tenant is a live person, the waiver for personal injury would affect only that person and not his or her employees. For that reason, landlords may require an indemnity, which is discussed below (page 63).

Thus, the waiver of subrogation should apply to the extent of the other party's property insurance (which should be described and should be adequate to cover possible losses). If, for example, the lease requires the landlord to carry property insurance on a full replacement cost basis (discussed on page 58), the waiver should apply to the extent of insurance required to be carried, but if the lease does not expressly require the landlord to carry such insurance, the waiver should apply to an amount of proceeds that the landlord would have recovered if "all-risk" property insurance were carried on a full replacement cost basis without coinsurance (see explanation on page 58). Obviously the same principle applies regarding the tenant's insurance. Nearly all leases require the tenant to insure its contents. Not as many require the landlord to insure its property. Appropriate provision should also be made in the event that the party owning the property carries a large deductible or self-insures for a property loss.

In short, the waiver of claims and the waiver of subrogation should eliminate fault as a factor in connection with the payment for a loss and place the risk on the party that owns the property who is in the position to carry property insurance.[7]

The amounts and kinds of property insurance to be required should vary with the nature of the insured property. The lease should discuss the following matters:

- contents insurance
- property insurance on the building
- proceeds available to rebuild
- rent insurance
- other insurance issues

Contents Insurance

Optimally, the lease should require the tenant to insure all contents, trade fixtures, machinery, equipment, furniture, and furnishings in the premises

---

7. The property owner may contract with the other party to carry the property insurance. This occurs when a net lease requires the tenant to purchase the property insurance on the building.

on a replacement cost basis under Special Form coverage insurance. "Special Form" coverage insures what used to be known as "all-risk" insurance, which was confusing because it did not really cover all risks, but every risk except for certain excluded risks, which were specified in the policy. In other words, it was not all-risk insurance after all.

In a lease that contains waivers of claims and mutual waivers of subrogation rights, the landlord wants this clause to ensure that the tenant has adequate insurance on its own property. If the tenant is actually carrying the required insurance and collects for any insured loss from its own insurance carrier, it has no economic reason to bring an action against the landlord even if the loss arises from the landlord's negligence; meanwhile, the waiver of the right of subrogation protects the landlord from suit by the tenant's insurance carrier.

Property Insurance on the Building

In a multi-tenant building, the landlord customarily carries the building's property insurance, whereas in a single-tenant building, the tenant sometimes carries the building insurance, naming the landlord as the insured.

When the landlord does carry the insurance in industrial/warehouse buildings, it pays the premium and usually passes all or some of the cost to its tenants. In office buildings and in shopping centers, the cost of building insurance is typically an "operating expense," or a "common area charge," which is passed through, in whole or in part, to the tenants. The building coverage may be broad or narrow; it may include only standard fire and extended coverage insurance, or it may include Special Form coverage. Usually, the landlord insures the entire building, including leasehold improvements. But sometimes the landlord insures only the shell of the building, and the tenant insures its own leasehold improvements. In my judgment, it is better for both parties (and certainly for the landlord's mortgagee) if the landlord undertakes to rebuild the entire building to its prior condition, and insures on that basis.

If the tenant is obligated under the lease to repair or restore following damage or destruction of the building (which is not unusual in net leases of a fairly long duration), the lease customarily provides that the proceeds needed for rebuilding will be made available to the tenant. If the tenant is not obligated to rebuild, the lease will generally specify the conditions under which a landlord must do so. It should be noted that in either event, the landlord's mortgage may provide that the lender has the right to apply insurance proceeds to pay down the indebtedness, rather than to make the proceeds available to rebuild.

Proceeds Available to Rebuild

Unfortunately, this is an area that does not receive much attention until after a fire or other insurable casualty has actually occurred. Leases typically require that the insurance proceeds be payable to the landlord, subject to a standard mortgage clause in the event that the premises are mortgaged to secure the landlord's indebtedness. The standard mortgage clause requires the insurance company to pay the proceeds to the lender. Whether the lender makes the insurance proceeds available so that the landlord (or the tenant, if so provided in the lease) can rebuild the premises depends on the terms of the mortgage. The first draft of most mortgages provides that if there is a fire or other casualty, the proceeds are to be paid to the lender, who may then apply the proceeds to pay down the loan or to restore the property. (It is beyond the scope of this book, but I strongly argue that the lender should, in most cases, be obligated to make the proceeds available to restore.) If a proposed lease is to be in place before the building is mortgaged, the parties to the lease, and particularly the tenant's broker, should make sure that the mortgage will provide that the insurance proceeds will be made available to rebuild—provided, of course, that the lease remains in full force and effect. That is easier said than done since the mortgage may not be negotiated until some time after the lease is signed and the broker has by then moved on to other deals. In that situation, however, the tenant's broker should educate his or her client. When the tenant is asked to sign a subordination, non-disturbance, and attornment agreement (see pages 41-44), it can seek to negotiate a provision in that agreement to the effect that the proceeds will be made available to rebuild the tenant's premises. Obviously, the tenant may need some economic clout to get such a provision, but that is the only time it may get the relief it requires.

If the mortgage is in place before the lease is signed, the tenant's broker should ask the tenant's lawyer to review the mortgage to determine if that document provides for the proceeds to be made available. If it does not, and if again the tenant has sufficient economic clout, the tenant can make the lease conditioned on obtaining a non-disturbance agreement that will require the lender to make the proceeds available to rebuild, subject to customary conditions such as the landlord not being in default under the loan documents or there being enough time left in the term of the loan, or the landlord making up any shortfall in the insurance proceeds. If the protection required by the tenant is not forthcoming, the tenant should seek the right to terminate the lease before any money is spent on construction.

If the lender has not agreed in the loan documents or, as to a particular tenant in a non-disturbance agreement, to make the proceeds available to rebuild, and if the landlord cannot obtain such an agreement at the time of a casualty, the landlord should have a right to terminate its tenant leases (otherwise, it would be in default under the leases). However, the tenant may not get a comparable right to terminate.

It is critically important to the landlord that tenants not be able to terminate their leases merely because of a fire or other casualty. If the leases are terminated, the lenders will certainly not make the insurance proceeds available for the rebuilding of the property (and that will no doubt be stated in the loan documents as an exception to the lender's obligation to make them available). The landlord would then be in an untenable position, especially if the building is only partly damaged, because any proceeds that the landlord receives would probably not be enough to pay off the loan, the debt service payment obligation would continue without reduction or abatement, and the landlord would have little or no income from which to service the debt. The landlord would have to go into the mortgage market, possibly in a higher interest rate market, with a half-destroyed building, to borrow funds to pay off the old debt and to rebuild the building to be able to re-lease it on a speculative basis. Of course, the tenant should be able to terminate if the landlord defaults in its obligation to rebuild (or to make the proceeds available to the tenant to rebuild if the tenant is obligated to do the restoration), or if the lender does not make the proceeds available.

Rent Insurance

The party that purchases the property insurance can, for a reasonable additional premium, buy coverage that will pay continuing expenses (like rent and taxes) during the period that the leased premises are untenantable (which means unfit for the purpose for which they are leased). If the lease is a net lease in which the rent is not abated, the insurance proceeds will not be paid. If the lease is silent on rent abatement, the tenant's broker should find out whether rent insurance proceeds will be paid, because the law in most states provides that rent will not abate in that case. In those states, rent abates only if the lease expressly provides for abatement. If rent does not abate, either because the lease so provides or because there is no provision in the lease and the law of the state is that it does not, then the insurance company will probably assert that there is no loss to the landlord and, accordingly, there should be no proceeds of rent loss insurance. If, however, the rent does abate as a result of the fire or other casualty, the landlord must be certain that he or she receives insurance proceeds to be able to continue to pay debt service and taxes.

Many leases provide that rent does not abate if the tenant caused the loss. If that is the case, the insurance company may have a defense to paying the proceeds of the rent loss insurance. Such a provision is intended to punish the tenant, but it does not really benefit the landlord. It only benefits the insurance company, which does not have to pay a claim for which it was actually compensated in its premium. If the tenant does not have business income insurance (often called "business interruption insurance"), the tenant will probably be unable to pay the rent while it is out of business because of the loss. Thus, a provision that says rent does not abate if the tenant caused the loss makes no sense at all since it punishes the landlord, as well as the tenant—and perhaps even more than the tenant.

Business Income Insurance

If all or a part of the premises are rendered untenantable and the lease does not terminate, the tenant may be forced to move out of the premises, move into other premises on a temporary basis, set up its operation and pay rent there, and then move out of the other premises and reoccupy the original leased premises when the repair or restoration is completed. If the rent does not abate, the tenant will continue to have to pay the rent as well. All of that will, of course, involve considerable expense that the tenant may cover business interruption and extra expenses by means of so-called "business income insurance." Most leases are silent about tenants' business income insurance. Tenants may argue, in negotiating for a right to terminate, that moving out and moving back in involves tremendous inconvenience and trauma, but the landlord's response must be that both landlord and tenant suffer from a casualty and that so long as the economic loss can be covered by business income insurance, the tenant should not have a right to terminate the lease. The problem of the retail tenant is more difficult than the problem of other tenants because comparable store premises may simply not be available in the same market. However, tenants can insure against loss of profits.

Loss Payable

Occasionally, when the lease requires the tenant to carry the building property insurance, the tenant may seek to negotiate that insurance proceeds be payable to both parties "as their interest may appear." However, the proceeds of the building property insurance should be payable only to the landlord. After all, the landlord does own the building. If the landlord is having a dispute with the tenant, the landlord does not want to be required to get the tenant's endorsement on the insurance proceeds check. Likewise, the tenant wants to be certain that the landlord's signature is not required on the check for its contents insurance proceeds.

If the tenant is required to rebuild leasehold improvements or alterations, and to insure them separately, it may want to be a payee of the insurance check for those items. On the other hand, the installed leasehold improvements do belong to the landlord, and they are subject to the lien of the landlord's mortgage. In that situation, the tenant's insurance should include a standard mortgage clause. I have serious issues with provisions in leases that require tenants to insure their leasehold improvements and alterations, which will be discussed below (see page 65).

Adjustment of Loss

It takes considerable time to adjust the loss after a fire or other casualty in a commercial building. The loss may be adjusted by the insurance carrier or by a public adjuster; it may be contested and involve lengthy disputes. Until the adjustment process is almost completed, the party obligated to rebuild does not know the extent of the proceeds available to rebuild and accordingly cannot make binding commitments. Once it can start planning, it must have plans and specifications drawn and find and negotiate with a contractor to perform the work.

Many leases give the party required to rebuild 60 days to accomplish the necessary steps prior to the commencement of the repair or rebuilding. That is an extremely short time for the landlord to adjust the loss, have the reconstruction designed, hire contractors, and be prepared to start construction. However tenants, who may be out of business, argue for the shortest possible time, and that is how it often ends up.

Replacement Cost, Actual Cash Value, and Coinsurance

If someone insures a building for its actual cash value, the insurance proceeds are limited to the building's replacement cost at the time of the loss minus physical depreciation (usually estimated at 1 percent for each year of the building's age). Assume that a 20-year-old building with a replacement cost of $10 million is insured for that amount on an actual cash value basis and is totally destroyed. The insurance carrier may assert that the physical depreciation is 20 percent, or $2 million, and that the net proceeds of the insurance are limited to $8 million. Obviously this leaves the landlord with less than he needs to rebuild the building.

If, however, the insurance is written on a full replacement cost basis, the insurer makes no deduction for physical depreciation, and the insured is entitled to receive the full cost of replacement (provided the insured has accurately estimated and purchased coverage for the actual replacement cost and subject, of course, to deductibles).

Many policies are written with 100 percent coinsurance clauses. That means the insurance company pays 100 percent of the loss, assuming, of course, that the amount of insurance carried is enough to pay the loss and that the insurance is carried on a replacement cost basis. This is appropriate if the insured has not underestimated the replacement cost. If the insured is carrying less insurance than is required to replace the building, not only would the underinsuring insurance buyer collect less than the building's replacement cost in the case of a total destruction but also would collect less than the actual cost of repairing in the event of a partial destruction. Here is how it works. If an owner insures the same $10 million building for $6 million at 100 percent coinsurance on a replacement cost basis and the building is totally destroyed, the insurance company is obligated to pay only the face amount of the policy. If, however, the loss is a partial rather than a total loss, the insurance company would pay only 60 percent of the actual loss because the owner's insurance was only 60 percent of the replacement cost. The insurance company would pay only $600,000 of a $1 million loss, even though that payment is significantly less than the $6 million face amount of the policy.

An insurance buyer can avoid the coinsurance problem by purchasing a policy with an "agreed amount endorsement." This endorsement is not a confirmation by the insurance company that the amount of the insurance is adequate; it is merely an agreement by the insurance company that the coinsurance result described above will not apply and that the insurance company will pay 100 percent of any partial loss, provided it is not in excess of the face amount of the policy. Obviously, such an endorsement is important to both parties to a lease.

To reduce the likelihood of underinsurance, it may be appropriate to provide in the lease for a periodic insurance appraisal, and should also specify who is obligated to pay for that appraisal.

Uninsured Risks

Although it is possible to insure against most casualty risks, certain risks, such as flood and earthquake, are not covered by Special Form policies. If a property is in a flood-risk area, flood insurance is usually available through an agency of the U.S. government. Earthquake insurance, on the other hand, may either be unavailable or may be very expensive, even in low-earthquake-risk areas. Unless there is a specific exclusion in the lease, the party obligated under the lease to rebuild following a casualty has contractually obligated himself to rebuild, even in the event of an uninsured casualty. That should certainly be considered in the negotiations.

Liability Insurance

Most liability situations in real estate do not arise because an act by one party to the lease results in damage to property of the other party. Those situations are covered by the waiver of claims and waiver of the right of subrogation discussed above (see page 50). Liability situations usually arise because some real person is injured or because a third party's property is damaged. Injury or damage can occur within the premises or in a common area. To avoid the risk of not suing the right party, the injured party customarily asserts a claim or files suit against all the people having an interest in the property. To prevent gaps in insurance coverage that may result in liability being imposed on an uninsured party, the system of requiring insurance naming another party as an additional insured has evolved. Still, because of the substantial problems that may arise if an injury to a person is uninsured, the parties frequently duplicate insurance, especially in a multi-tenant building.

In a single-occupant building in which the tenant also has the exclusive use and occupancy of the parking lot and the balance of the real estate, the tenant's liability insurance should cover the entire property, and the landlord may decide not to carry liability insurance at all. If the landlord does carry this insurance, its cost probably would be reduced because it would be considered secondary rather than primary coverage. In multi-tenant buildings, landlords should carry liability insurance because injuries occurring in the common areas may not be covered by the tenant's liability insurance unless they result from the tenant's acts. Of course, each party should carry liability insurance covering its own acts off the property.

Additional or Named Insured

Landlords' lease forms customarily require the tenant to carry liability insurance that names the landlord (as well as the landlord's mortgagee) as an additional insured for injuries to a person or damages to property that occur on the leased premises. This can generally be achieved without the payment of additional premiums, presumably because the tenant has exclusive control of the premises and because if negligence is involved, it will be the tenant's rather than the landlord's. Thus, if a person is injured on the leased premises, the tenant's liability insurance will respond to that loss, whether it is caused by the landlord or the tenant.

"Additional insured" should not be confused with "named insured." While there is some question (due to judicial decisions) about the scope of the coverage for the landlord if it is included in the tenant's policy as an "additional insured," it is clear that if the landlord is a "named insured," it is actually one of the parties covered by the insurance provided for in the policy. While the landlord who is a named insured is jointly liable with the tenant for the payment of the premium, the lease will provide that the tenant must pay for the coverage. Most tenants strongly object to including the landlord as a "named insured," particularly tenants that have policies covering more than one location. Still, it is sometimes agreed to in single-tenant buildings because the tenant will not have to pay for its own liability insurance and for a separate policy for the landlord's.

Insurance Limits

Leases customarily specify the amount of liability insurance that the tenant must carry. The required amounts have increased over the years. Given the phenomenon of rising judgments, at some point during the term of a long or extended lease, the specified amount may prove inadequate. A well-drafted lease, therefore, gives the landlord the right, on notice, to require the tenant to increase the liability insurance limits if, in the landlord's reasonable judgment, the specified amount is insufficient to protect the various parties. This requirement protects the tenant as well as the landlord, although it does place the decision in the landlord's hands, to which the tenant, its broker, or its lawyer may object. An alternative is to relate required amounts of liability insurance to amounts customarily carried in the geographic area. It is not wise to tie increases in liability insurance coverage to increases in the consumer price index because changes in that index are not necessarily related to increases in judgment amounts.

Combined Single Limit per Occurrence and Aggregate

Liability insurance used to be written with separate amounts for personal injury to one person, for personal injury to more than one person in one occurrence, and for property damage. Now liability insurance is written on the basis of a combined single limit per occurrence and aggregate. This means that there is one limit for the sum of all claims, demands, or actions that arise in a single occurrence, whether those claims, demands, or actions arise out of personal injury or property damage.

The word "aggregate" that the insurance companies tack on to the end of the policy description means that they will not pay more than the aggregate limit in any one policy year. For example, a policy may be written with a $1 million occurrence limit and a $2 million aggregate. If there were three losses of $800,000 each during the policy year, the insurance company would pay only $400,000 toward the third loss. It is possible to obtain an endorsement that specifies that "aggregate" shall apply separately to each location owned or rented by the tenant. It is obviously in the interest of both landlord and tenant to obtain such an endorsement whenever the tenant has more than one location so that no risk is left uncovered.

Occurrence and Claims-Made Coverage

Yet another wrinkle arises from time to time in connection with liability policies. A change in general liability coverage has been imported by the insurance industry from products liability and malpractice coverage. Although it is not common, liability coverage occasionally is written on a claims-made rather than on an occurrence basis. In the occurrence basis situation, a claim is covered if the loss occurred while the policy was in effect, even if the claim is made after the policy expires. A claims-made policy provides coverage for claims made while the policy is in effect even if the events on which the claims are based occurred before the particular policy was purchased. Liability insurance written on a claims-made rather than on an occurrence basis can cause gaps in coverage. Assume, for example, that someone is injured on the premises during the last year of the lease term. The tenant moves out at the end of the term and does not continue to maintain claims-made liability insurance because it is going out of business.[8] The injured party sues the landlord and tenant after the lease term ends. The tenant's liability insurance no longer covers the loss because the claim was made after the term of the insurance expired. Unfortunately, in this situation, the landlord's problem would not be solved by a provision in the lease requiring the tenant to continue to carry liability insurance on a claims-made basis after the lease has expired. Even if the tenant remains in business, there is no efficient way for the landlord to police or enforce that obligation.

Most tenants who carry insurance on a claims-made basis are large companies that own or lease numerous properties. Although such large companies are likely to remain in business and to continue to carry insurance on a claims-made basis until after the statute of limitations period shall have expired to cover incidents that occurred during the lease term, the landlord has no assurance that this will be the case. The only way a landlord can adequately protect itself in this situation is to carry its own liability insurance. There is, obviously, a cost in doing that, and landlords expect tenants to bear the cost. It is doubtful that tenants would agree.

Indemnity

Another way for parties to a lease to protect themselves from liability for injuries to a person or damages to property is by the use of indemnities. Leases typically require tenant indemnities to protect the landlord. Liability insurance policies usually contain "contractual liability" language. That means the policy covers liability assumed by the tenant under the lease for injuries to a person or damages to the property of others, provided the assumption of liability occurs before the injury or damage. An indemnity, unlike the insurance, is not usually limited in amount; thus, the tenant is assuming liability to pay a judgment against the landlord that might be greater than the coverage required in the lease or the amount of the tenant's actual liability insurance limits (if greater than what the lease requires).

---

8. If the tenant is continuing in business elsewhere, it will most likely be continuing the insurance coverage, which is fine, unless the tenant switches to occurrence insurance; going out of business is the major risk for landlords.

Indemnities frequently cover more than liability claims. They may relate to claims for damages arising out of the failure of the tenant to perform the terms of the lease or to pay for construction work in the premises. Insurance would not cover those other claims.

Although tenants frequently request that the indemnity exclude losses arising from the landlord's negligent or willful act, this does not seem appropriate if the tenant's liability insurance names the landlord as an additional insured or if the indemnity is covered by the contractual liability provision in the tenant's policy. On the other hand, it seems reasonable that if the landlord's negligence or willful act causes a loss that exceeds the amount of liability insurance, the landlord, and not the tenant, should be responsible for the excess over the insurance coverage.

Tenants frequently request that landlords indemnify them against the landlord's acts. Landlords confront several problems in giving indemnities that are as broad as the indemnities that they require from tenants. A landlord should not indemnify a tenant against events that the tenant, but not the landlord, is required to be insured against; a landlord that does agree to such an indemnity could assume liability for which it has no liability insurance coverage. Any landlord's indemnity should carefully exclude liability arising on the premises or for losses caused by the tenant. Essentially, this means that if the landlord is insuring the common areas, the landlord can indemnify the tenant (and obtain contractual liability insurance coverage for such indemnity) for the landlord's acts relative to the common areas.

Other Issues
Goods Owned by Third Parties
Landlords that lease premises to users who store or sell products belonging to third parties—such as public warehouses, third-party logistics companies, warehouses used by common carriers, or retail tenants that accept goods on consignment—have special problems. The waiver of claims by the tenant does not protect the landlord from liability for damages to goods owned by third parties caused by the landlord's negligence. The value of those goods may well exceed the liability insurance carried by the landlord, especially since the landlord has no way of knowing the value in the first place, so the landlord has no practical way to protect itself. A warehouse operator

or the retailer who accepts consignment merchandise can put in its contract a limitation of its liability, but that does not benefit the landlord. The landlord can insist on an indemnity from the tenant (and adequate insurance), but that is expensive and may not be agreeable to the tenant. I can offer no easy solution to this problem, but brokers for both the landlord and the tenant should be aware of it; not many lawyers are.

Tenant Improvements and Alterations

Many leases require the tenant to insure its alterations to the premises, and some require the tenant to insure the initial tenant improvements. In my judgment, this is not appropriate. The landlord should, and usually does, insure the building as improved. It is, most likely, required to do so in its mortgage because the lender does not want to have to chase a number of tenants to get the insurance proceeds so it can systematically make them available to rebuild. The tenant is paying for the landlord's property insurance, either in its base rent or in additional rent. If, in addition, it is required to carry property insurance on its alterations or leasehold improvements, it is paying twice for the same insurance, which is in neither party's interest.

Sometimes, when representing tenants, I get the Taj Mahal argument. Why, it questions, should all the tenants pay if a particular tenant spends an enormous sum to improve its space? There are two answers to that. Unless it is the major tenant, the cost of the insurance will probably not increase that much. If there is a substantial increase in the cost of the insurance, however, the landlord will usually require the tenant to pay that increase as a condition to consenting to the improvement. Since most tenants will not ordinarily negotiate to share in the benefit of other tenants paying a greater share of the landlord's insurance cost, the landlord will in all probability not reduce the other tenants' share of the cost of insurance, so the landlord may double dip (keeping the excess for itself).

Self-Insurance

Many financially strong tenants seek the right to self-insure. This is certainly understandable since the net worth of those companies may exceed that of some insurance carriers and those tenants may consider the insurance an unnecessary expense. In the alternative, those tenants may seek the right to carry insurance with very large deductibles, and insure only catastrophic risks.

Tenants' self-insurance creates risks for landlords. First, what if the strong tenant assigns the lease to a weak one? The right to self-insure should not pass to the assignee. Second, what if the strong tenant suddenly becomes a weak one, as happened so often during the recession during which once mighty General Motors sought bankruptcy reorganization and a government bail-out. The right should end if the tenant does not maintain a certain tangible net worth.[9] Third, the landlord was counting on the tenant's property insurance to give effect to the waiver of claims and the waiver of the right of subrogation. How does the landlord protect itself against suits for negligent damage to the tenant's property? The lease should specifically provide that the self-insurance is deemed to be insurance for the purpose of those waivers.

Summary

I have used a lot of space in this book and spent a lot of your time on insurance-related issues. What you have learned here will, I believe, be very useful in your profession. I caution you, however: there is still much I have not covered, and the insurance business, like the real estate business, is not static. What is called Special Form today may well have another name tomorrow, or even by the time you are reading this book. In teaching the course for SIOR (see the preface, page vii), Steve Podolsky emphasized the importance of befriending a good insurance agent, whose brain you may pick for information and advice. The same advice would apply to any number of experts in other fields that affect tenant brokerage.

Assignment and Subletting

First I would like to clear up a possible misconception about assignment and subletting. When Steve Podolsky and I taught that course and we asked

---

9. I prefer using "tangible net worth" to plain old "net worth," which might include goodwill or other intangibles that do not have ready market value.

what the difference was between the two, many brokers said that under an assignment the assignor is released from further obligations under the lease. WRONG ANSWER! The assignor is not automatically released. That only happens if the assigned lease provides that, or if the landlord agrees at the time to such a release.

So what is the difference between the two?

Under the law, if a tenant transfers all of its interest in the lease and the premises, it is an assignment, no matter what it is called. If the tenant reserves some interest, even if the document is called an assignment, it is actually a sublease. In other words, if the tenant "subleases" the entire premises for the entire term, it is really an assignment. That is why subleases generally end a day or so before the tenant's term ends. Similarly, if the tenant "assigns" the lease but reserves a right of reentry—the right to take back the space and resume its position as the tenant—if the assignee defaults, that is considered, under the law, a sublease. In other words, if there is litigation and it is material whether the document is a sublease or an assignment, those principles will apply. While it is important to keep those principles in the back of our minds, that is probably where they belong, because, in practice, most "subleases" are really subleases and most assignments are really assignments.

Under an assignment, the tenant parts with all of its rights under the lease (although it remains liable for the nonperformance of obligations unless it is expressly released). The assignment creates a direct relationship between the landlord and the assignee as if they had done the lease directly. We call this "privity of contract." While assignments of part of the premises are legally possible, this is almost never done because of the impracticality of dividing rights and obligations between the assignor and the assignee. Since the assignment is based on the terms and conditions of the existing lease, the assignee is obligated to pay rent at the rate specified in the lease. Hence, assignments are not generally used when the tenant proposes to dispose of the space at a lower rent than it is paying the landlord. There are ways to deal with this, however, as I will discuss (see page 68).

Although I have discussed the nature of the sublease (see pages 30-37), there is more to be said about it. Generally, subleases are used when the tenant desires to dispose of all or part of its premises for less than all of its term, or even if it is for all of the term (minus one day), at a rental rate or on other terms different from the original lease. The sublease is, in effect, a new lease between the tenant (as sublandlord) and the subtenant. The privity of contract is not between the subtenant and the landlord (known as the prime landlord, master landlord or overlandlord), but between the sublandlord and the subtenant. The subtenant does not have the right to sue the prime landlord if it does not perform its obligations, even if the subtenant is damaged by that. It must have the sublandlord do so, for its benefit, and that should be provided for in the sublease document.

In the assignment situation, if the assignee defaults and the landlord sues the original tenant, that tenant may be able to proceed against the assignee under an indemnity or other agreement in the assignment to perform the obligations under the lease. However, the original tenant does not have the right to kick the assignee out of the space, to resume its position as tenant and possibly to assign the lease to another assignee or sublease the premises. As I wrote above, if the original tenant reserves a right of reentry, which it may do, it will be deemed a sublandlord under a sublease, which may have other consequences. In the sublease situation, the tenant/sublandlord may in fact evict the subtenant and resume full occupancy of the premises, or at least be in a position to sublease the premises to another subtenant and thus mitigate its damages.

Assignments are often (but not always) used when a tenant is selling its business and is transferring the lease as one of the assets being sold. As I said, subleases are usually used to dispose of unneeded space.

What if your client wishes to assign the lease and get out of the picture completely (perhaps the credit of the assignee is sufficient that the landlord is willing to release your client from future obligations), but the assignee is unwilling to pay the amount of rent specified in the lease. Here is a handy solution to the problem that I have used (and it is also handy in a sub-sublease situation, to avoid over-complication). I provide for the assignor to agree to pay the difference between the lease rent and the rent the assignee is willing to pay. The entire difference may be paid in advance, but at a discounted rate, or it may be paid monthly in advance—or quarterly or yearly, whatever the parties decide—and the obligation to pay may be secured by a letter of credit from a bank. Although the obligation of the bank under a letter of credit must be secured, by deposit of some assets of the assignor in this case, such letters of credit are not expensive.

Why might a tenant wish to assign its lease or sublease to all or a portion of its premises? Most tenants, when they lease space, expect to occupy all of it for the duration of the lease. There are exceptions, of course (as there are to almost every situation described in this book). A tenant may be leasing more space than it needs at the time and intends to sublease the portion it does not need so it may grow into it; thus it is "warehousing" the extra space. Or a tenant may be in some business where it has a close working relationship with another entity and wants that entity close.

More commonly, however, the reasons for disposing of the lease or the premises arise from changes in the tenant's business. The tenant may outgrow the space and desire to lease larger premises; a retail tenant may feel that its business would be more successful at a different location; the tenant may have suffered a business reversal and wishes to downsize or close altogether; and, of course, the tenant may sell its business and have no further need for the space.

Leases generally provide that the landlord's consent is required for a transfer, whether it be by assignment or sublease. If the lease is silent, then the rule of law is that the tenant's interest in the lease or the premises may be transferred without the landlord's consent. As you would expect, very few leases are silent on the matter. The real issue is whether the landlord must act reasonably. The law varies from state to state as to whether, if the lease is silent on reasonableness, the landlord must be reasonable. For that reason, it is customary for tenants to insist that the lease provide that the landlord must act reasonably.[10] What does "reasonable" mean? It is a rather vague standard, but one frequently used in many leases and in connection with many other provisions of leases and contracts. It means that courts (or arbitrators) must decide whether, under all the circumstances, the landlord properly denied the right to transfer.

Many leases have a list of standards as to which a denial or consent will be deemed reasonable. The following are some of the frequently seen standards:

---

10. See footnote 8 on page 37.

1. The tenant may not be in default under the lease.
2. The manner of the subtenant's use of the premises after the subletting or assignment, even if consistent with the use clause, may not be detrimental to the property.
3. The proposed subtenant or assignee must be acceptable, financially and otherwise.
4. The proposed subtenant or assignee may not be a government agency.
5. The proposed subtenant or assignee may not be a tenant in the building.
6. The proposed subtenant or assignee may not then be negotiating with the landlord for a lease on the property and may not have negotiated with the landlord for space on the property within the prior 12 months.
7. The proposed rental rate in the sublease may not be lower than that quoted by the landlord for comparable space on the property.

Let us consider these standards. As to number 1, why should the tenant not have the right to cure the default (if it is curable) in connection with the transfer? The landlord is made whole and the tenant may proceed to realize his objective in making the transfer. Number 2 refers to the possible change in the way the subtenant plans to operate in premises, which may be detrimental. That seems fair. As to number 3, how is acceptability to be determined? If the transferee has the financial capacity to perform its obligations, it should not have to be Apple, Inc. And what does "otherwise" mean? Still, this language can be made more specific and the concept survive. What about number 4? We have already learned about the pros and cons of government leases (see page 33), so we can see why some landlords would not want them in the building. However, this limitation might not be appropriate in Washington, D.C., or a state capital.

Numbers 5, 6, and 7 present real difficulties for tenants. I can understand that a landlord does not want the tenant competing with it for other tenants, but if the space proposed to be transferred is the perfect space for the prospect (who may be the next-door neighbor), why should the tenant be prevented from subleasing to it, especially if the landlord does not have other suitable space for that party? How is the tenant supposed to know that the landlord is negotiating with the prospective tenant? And if the negotiations between the landlord and the prospective tenant broke off, what legitimate claim does the landlord have to that prospect? Finally as to number 7, most subleases are for a lower rent than the tenant is paying, let alone the rent being quoted for other space on the property, which, except in a down market, is likely to be higher than the tenant's rent; that is essentially a prohibition on subleasing.

Notice that none of the standards above address the change in the permitted use of the premises. That may be because the lease will say that the transferee is bound by all of the provisions of the lease, including purpose or use clause. The tenant's broker would be wise to protect his or her client's right to transfer the lease for a different use, although the landlord and its broker will be concerned about what a new use might be. In a shopping center situation, for example, the landlord is concerned about tenant mix, or possible violations of exclusive rights given to other tenants. A retail landlord might have negotiated a low percentage rent rate (see page 129) suitable for the particular tenant, but the transferee might be selling products that typically generate a higher rate. An industrial/warehouse landlord might be concerned about a use that would risk greater damage to the building. An office landlord might be concerned about a much higher traffic user.

Another common means by which a landlord seeks to limit its risk of being deemed unreasonable is to limit the tenant's remedies. Ordinarily, if a court holds that a landlord unreasonably withheld consent, it could award damages to the tenant for loss of the benefit of the transfer. To be fair to landlords, some decisions are pretty close calls, and landlords may be induced to consent when it feels it has grounds not to do so because of the risk of litigation and possible damages. Thus it is not uncommon to see leases that limit the tenant's remedies to declaratory judgment or injunction. In other words, if the landlord withholds consent, the tenant may sue and ask the court to determine that the landlord was unreasonable (such suits are permitted in most but not all states) or to enjoin the landlord from withholding consent. No damages may be awarded. The problem for the tenant is that any legal proceeding is time-consuming and by the time the court decides, the prospect will have moved on. With due regard to the landlord's concerns, the remedy proposed is no remedy at all, but it is very difficult to come up with an expedited way to determine reasonableness, and landlords are often simply unwilling to risk a damage award.

There are other ways in which landlords seek to control transfers. You may recall my mentioning some leases made in the 1960s that were 20 years in duration and as to which tenants had the right to assign or sublease pretty freely (see page 23). Well, from that experience came two new concepts: recapture and sharing of profits.

Recapture means that if a tenant proposes to assign its lease, or sublease the premises or a portion thereof, the landlord may, instead of consenting, terminate the lease or, in the case of a partial sublease, the portion proposed to be subleased. In the termination of a portion situation, the space is divided and the rent reduced. In any case, the landlord may lease the premises recaptured to the prospect or hold the premises for leasing to third parties at the market rent at the time. The tenant's obligations are eliminated or reduced, as the case may be, but the landlord, not the tenant, makes the profit from leasing the premises. Of course, if the landlord has reasonable grounds for withholding consent, it may elect, instead of exercising its right to terminate, to withhold consent and keep the tenant "on the hook," as we say.

There are certain situations in which the tenant has a legitimate objection to the landlord's terminating the lease. For example, if the tenant is proposing to sell its business and is assigning the lease in that connection, a recapture by the landlord might prevent the sale. That exception should be negotiated in the lease at its inception.

Sharing of profits is not, during a downturn in the economy, a major concern, but it might be in inflationary times. Lease forms often provide that if the tenant is making a profit on the transfer, the entire profit goes to the landlord. This is not only unfair, it is foolish. If the tenant gets no portion of the profit, it has no incentive to negotiate a higher rent than it is paying the landlord. Neither party gets anything. A 50-50 split is where the compromise usually comes out. Again, the tenant is worried about how the profit is determined. There are usually expenses involved in finding a new tenant and making changes in the space. Should those expenses come out before the split? What if, as part of an assignment, the tenant is selling equipment or being reimbursed for the unamortized leasehold improvements or being paid for good will as part of the sale of the business or selling another location? That income is not profit from the transfer of the premises and should be excluded in the lease.

Most leases prohibit the transfer of option rights in connection with an assignment or subletting. Thus, if the lease is assigned two years before its expiration and the assignee is counting on the right to exercise an existing option in order to continue the business in the premises, it may find, on review of the lease, that option is not transferred with the assignment and it will have to negotiate an extension with the landlord. I can understand the landlord's position here; an option is a "one-way street" in that the only benefit the landlord gets is that the tenant is willing to sign the lease (which it might not do without the option). Options are discussed further below (see pages 85-87). On the other hand, the tenant may not be able to conclude the sale of the premises or the business because the option is not transferable.

Even if the option is transferable, another issue arises. As I noted above, the tenant remains liable under the lease if it assigns the lease. But what if it assigns the lease and the assignee exercises an option to extend or to take additional premises. Is the tenant liable for the obligations under the lease during the extended term or for the additional premises? I am confident that, in the absence of an agreement in the lease, the answer varies from state to state, but the landlord will certainly want the liability to continue on the grounds that the exercise of the option was a contingency anticipated in the original lease, and the tenant will certainly want it to end on the grounds that what the exercise of the option created was, in effect, a new deal. So if any option is transferable, this issue will have to be addressed by the parties, their brokers, and their lawyers.

Delivery of Possession, Construction, and Commencement Date

The issues under this heading vary, based not only on type of use but also on the condition of the premises and of the building of which the premises are a part. Thus the premises may exist in a completed building and are in move-in condition. Under those circumstances, it is customary to say that the premises shall be delivered in "as is, where is" condition, although I prefer to say, on behalf of landlords, "in their condition as of the execution and delivery of this lease, reasonable wear, and tear excepted." Note that if the landlord is doing any work whatsoever on the premises to prepare them for the tenant's occupancy, even if it is as simple as painting and carpeting, they are not being delivered in "as is, where is" condition, and the work to be performed should be described in the lease or in an exhibit attached to the lease (including who is to select the paint color or carpet design).

It is not uncommon for the landlord to have to perform work before delivering possession of the premises to the tenant. That work may involve building a new building, which may be a build-to-suit where the premises are move-in ready, or it may simply be four walls and a roof where the tenant does the final build-out for its own use. More commonly, the landlord's work will be in an existing building and may range from checking and repairing the mechanical systems, or cleaning out debris or equipment left by the prior tenant, to construction to prepare existing premises for the new tenant's use, or at least for that tenant's own construction. In an industrial/warehouse building, the landlord's work might consist of constructing some office space, or even demolishing the prior tenant's office space. The landlord might be running additional power to the premises, constructing a demising wall to separate the premises from other space, or erecting interior walls and running power or heated and chilled water to a single location, leaving it to the tenant to do the finishing work in the space, distribute the power, and convert heated and chilled water to actual heating and air conditioning. In the latter situation, the landlord is commonly said to deliver a vanilla box to the tenant. The tenant's obligation to complete the space is usually described in considerable detail in the lease or, more commonly, in a work letter agreement, attached as an exhibit to the lease. The possibilities are nearly endless.

Retail users often have very specific requirements for the conduct of their business and desire to do the build-out of their space themselves. Chain retailers may have a template design and use the same architects and designers all over the country. They are happy to receive a vanilla box so that they may build the space to their specifications. Retailers, generally, may be very specific about what the landlord is constructing, as well as the timing of the work, since they may want to be open in time for the Christmas season, and if they miss it, they do not want to have to open during that season because they are so busy..

Of course, in each of those situations, the deal may call for the landlord to build out the space to the tenant's specifications, in what is referred to as a "turnkey" build-out.

Leases and work letter agreements tend to be pretty specific about the landlord's required work and, since they are generally drafted for landlords, even more specific about the tenant's work, but they are often subject to considerable negotiation. What happens if the landlord is delayed in the performance of its work? What if the delay is caused by the tenant? What constitutes completion or, more commonly, substantial completion of landlord's work? How are disputes about whether the work is substantially completed to be resolved?

The landlord is obviously concerned about what will be built by the tenant in its building. It wants to see and approve plans and specifications; it wants to make certain that all legal requirements are met and that required permits and certificates of occupancy are obtained by the tenant. It is concerned that the contractors working in the building are reputable and qualified to perform the work, and that they will not damage the building or interfere with other tenants. The documents may require that the contractor employ union labor, particularly if the landlord uses union labor. The landlord wants to make certain that no mechanic's liens are filed against the building or, if they are filed, that the liens be contested promptly and properly and that the property is secured against an adverse decision in the contest. The landlord also wants to assure that the work is completed on schedule, so that the tenant may begin paying rent on time.

Who pays for the work is a critical economic issue. Typically, the landlord pays for the landlord's work. If the landlord is performing the work on a "turnkey" basis, the lease may cap the landlord's cost exposure, with the tenant required to pay any difference, either in the form of a rent increase or in cash (sometimes over time with an interest factor built in). When the tenant is performing its work, it may negotiate a construction allowance covering all or a portion of the cost of the work. Of course, the landlord is not paying a construction allowance out of the goodness of its heart (if it has one). The cost of the construction allowance (as well as other construction by the landlord) is factored into the rent payable by the tenant. The lease may specify that the construction allowance may be used only for actual hard and soft construction costs and not for furniture, fixtures, and equipment (FF&E), because the landlord wants its money to go into the building.[11] The lease may also specify that excess costs may not be applied as a rent credit, although in my judgment, that is unfair since the cost of the construction allowance is factored into the rent, and if the landlord does not fund the entire construction allowance and does not reduce the rent, it is getting the money twice.

So when does the lease commence? That is not such an easy question, either, since the lease may commence at different times for different purposes. Obviously, when the landlord delivers possession of the premises to the tenant, the lease starts for some purposes. The tenant is entitled to the possession to perform its work. It must, during that time, carry insurance, possibly pay for utilities, and perform other obligations. But has the "term" commenced? The "term" is defined as the period of years specified in the lease between what is usually referred to as the "commencement date" and the end of the lease. Often the term commencement date is the earlier of the date the tenant opens for business in the premises and the date for commencement specified in the lease (which may be a set number of days after the landlord delivers the premises with landlord's work substantially completed). Does the rent start on the term commencement date? Maybe yes and maybe no. If the tenant has negotiated a rent concession, such as six months of free rent, the rent commencement date will be later than the term commencement date, and certainly later than the delivery date. On the other hand, it is possible, although unusual, that the parties may provide that the rent will commence on the delivery date, or some other date—it is all a matter of the agreement of the parties.

Let me add a word about "as-built" plans, which are often required by the landlord after the tenant's work (or any alteration) is completed. There are two types of as-built plans. One is the set of working drawings marked

---

11. Hard costs are the actual costs of physical construction; soft costs are architectural and engineering fees, permits, and similar necessary related costs.

as construction proceeds to indicate construction changes from the original plans. If, for example, an electrical outlet cannot be located where shown on the working drawings, the actual location will be shown on the marked working drawings. The other as-built plans are those prepared by architects after the project has been completed. This is a time-consuming and expensive project and is generally not really needed by the landlord, who just wants to know what the premises look like after the work and does not need an expensive and fancy drawing. In any case, the lease should state which type of as-built plans is required.

Alterations

Alterations provisions present many of the same issues as initial leasehold improvements. The landlord wants to know and approve what is being performed in the premises, and that the alterations are legal; it wants to approve the contractor; it wants to make certain that the tenant can pay for the alterations and that the landlord will be protected from possible lien claims. But there are additional issues to be considered in connection with proposed alterations.

The landlord may want the right to perform the alterations itself, at the tenant's cost, using the landlord's own contractor. Certainly, if there is to be roof work, the landlord wants to make certain that there is no violation of any roof warranty and the best way to assure that is to have the landlord's roofing contractor perform the work. The landlord may have a legitimate concern that the tenant will contract with unqualified but inexpensive contractors (or use the tenant's own employees). On the other hand, the tenant is concerned about the cost of the work and can foresee that it will cost more money if the landlord does the alteration. If the landlord allows the tenant to perform the work with its own contractors or employees, the landlord may still want the right to monitor the work (for which it will certainly insist on receiving a fee). In any case, the tenant will want the right to perform redecorating or minor work without the hassle of the full-blown requirements typical in alterations sections. The parties will have to negotiate just what constitutes minor work, probably based on the cost of the work (with a limited yearly aggregate).

Another issue is what is to happen to the alterations at the end of the term. Usually the "surrender" provision of the lease (see page 117) deals with removal of alterations, but it seems to me that the alterations section is the proper place to deal with that issue. The tenant should request that the lease require the landlord to decide, when it consents to the alteration, whether the alterations must be removed by the tenant upon surrender. Sometimes landlords are willing to agree to that, but sometimes they feel that they cannot make the decision at that time because the value of the alteration at the end of the term will depend on whether it might be useful or detrimental to a succeeding tenant. If the landlord is willing to decide the issue when requested to approve the alteration, however, it is my view that the tenant should be required to ask for such a decision as part of its request for the approval of the alteration. After all, the landlord may forget that it must decide at that time, leaving the matter in a sort of limbo. In addition, it is in the tenant's interest to have the landlord decide not only whether it will require removal but also whether, instead, it will require that the alteration be left in place. The alteration may be useful to the tenant after removal and the tenant may want to know whether it can take the alteration with it. Needless to say, the landlord will require that the tenant repair any damage caused by the removal, and perhaps even that the tenant restore the premises to their condition prior to the making of the alteration.

Mechanic's Liens

Just about every state has mechanic's lien laws to protect the rights of contractors to be paid for construction. The problem is that the lien laws vary greatly from state to state. Any construction done on premises, whether it be initial leasehold improvements performed in accordance with a work letter agreement or as an alteration, may create a right of the contractor (or its subcontractors or material suppliers) to file a lien claim, the effect of which is to encumber to the property and, if the lien is held to be valid and the claim remains unpaid, to result in a foreclosure sale of the property.

You can easily see that this would be very damaging to the landlord, the other tenants, and to the tenant causing the lien itself. For that reason, leases tend to be very strict about preventing lien claims and, if any are filed, to require that they be satisfied right away.

However (and there seems always to be a "however" in this book), the lien claim may not be legitimate. The work may not have been done, or done satisfactorily. The contractor may, in fact, already have been paid, but claim payment for extras that were not authorized. The lien claim may have been filed too late or be defective for some other reason. There can be any number of defenses to the claim, and the tenant typically asks for a right to contest the lien claim, and not to be considered in default until the contest is resolved. In many states, the tenant would have the right to bond over the lien claim in court, so the lien claim is, from a title examination standpoint, discharged. In Illinois, where I practice, that procedure is not available, so we typically require the tenant to cause a title insurance company to insure over the lien claim (the title company would require an indemnity and a deposit of security to do so), or that the tenant deposit security with the landlord to assure that the claim, and all interest and costs, will be paid if the tenant loses the contest.

Maintenance

As I discussed above (see page 21), triple-net leases in single-tenant buildings frequently require the tenant to perform all maintenance (except for those items specifically reserved as the landlord's responsibility). I discussed those triple-net leases in terms of industrial/warehouse leasing, but single-tenant office or retail leases may also be triple net when the tenant performs all maintenance. In all those situations, it is typical for maintenance to include replacement of items or features that can no longer be repaired. It is important for the landlord to specify what items of replacement are the tenant's responsibility or are charged to the tenant because, in the absence of such specificity, a court might rule that, since replacements are typically a landlord function, the landlord will have to pay for them.

If the landlord has agreed to maintain roof and structure, both parties should understand the precise scope of the landlord's responsibility so that a clear line can be drawn between the duties of each of them. If the tenant is to repair the roof until it can no longer be repaired, how and when is it determined that the landlord must replace it? Does the roof include the structural portions that underlie the roof membrane? What about flashings and other components of the roof? As to structure, is the landlord's responsibility limited to conditions that arise due to defects in the original construction or does it include conditions resulting from deterioration? Who is responsible for tuck-pointing? What if the tenant's negligence or the nature of its use causes the problem? All these questions must be answered in the lease, and thus considered in the negotiation of the lease. It is obvious that the answers to the questions will have substantial economic impact on the parties.

Getting beyond roof and structure, a very contentious issue is the condition of HVAC equipment, particularly rooftop units. Usually the tenant will ask for the landlord to at least put that equipment in working condition before the lease commences. Beyond that, the tenant may agree to perform maintenance, but seek to have the landlord replace the equipment if that becomes necessary during the term. Those issues can lead to a lot of discussion about payment for the cost of replacement—with the tenant arguing that the new equipment will have a useful life after the lease is over, so the landlord should pay the entire cost, and the landlord arguing that the tenant has the benefit of the useful life of the existing equipment, so the tenant should pay the entire cost. Both arguments have some validity, so the parties usually reach some compromise about sharing the cost.

In a multi-tenant building leased on a net basis in which the landlord advances the cost of certain maintenance but the tenants reimburse the landlord for their share of those costs, the issues are essentially the same. In gross leases with stops, the landlord's maintenance obligations are spelled out, and the cost of landlord's performance is usually covered in operating expenses or common-area expenses. Here again, the parties will discuss what portion of the cost of repair or replacement of certain items should be charged to the tenant, and the parties may agree to amortize "capital" costs over the useful life of the item, with some interest factor, and with the tenant paying amortization only during the term of its lease (and any extensions).

Most leases provide that the tenant is obligated to maintain the interior of its premises (and in the case of single-tenant buildings, the exterior, as well). Disputes may arise as to underground pipes, and they are usually resolved by specifying that the tenant is responsible only for those that serve its premises. Most leases also provide that, unless the repair or replacement is to be paid for out of insurance proceeds, the tenant must repair or replace or pay for items that it or its contractors, suppliers, employees, or customers damage, even if those items were otherwise the responsibility of the landlord.

It is not unusual for the lease to require the tenant to arrange for a maintenance contract for certain equipment. HVAC equipment, for example, will have a much shorter life if it is not inspected and serviced regularly. The same applies to elevators and escalators, as failure to maintain may cost the landlord a lot of money after the lease is over.

Damage or Destruction

If a fire or other casualty occurs, the parties will rush to the lease to determine their rights and obligations; that may be the only time after its execution that the lease is taken out of the drawer. Except in a single-tenant lease in which the tenant has undertaken repair and restoration, the obligation to restore will be the landlord's. There will usually be a time period before the landlord is obligated to commence the restoration, and either an obligation to proceed with due diligence or to complete the restoration within a specified period of time. The lease will usually provide that the rent will abate while, and to the extent that, the premises are not usable by the tenant for the operation of its business.

Some leases provide that the landlord will restore the base building and that the tenant is obligated to restore the balance. This might mean that the landlord will again deliver a vanilla box to the tenant and the tenant has to rebuild its leasehold improvements, or it might mean that the landlord will restore to the condition prior to the performance of alterations by the tenant, but that the tenant has to restore its own alterations. Usually this is tied in with the tenant's obligation to carry insurance on its improvements. In my view, these requirements are inappropriate for the reasons stated above (see page 65). Typically mortgages require the landlord to insure the building and to have the insurance proceeds payable to the lender so the lender may apply them to pay down the loan or to the restoration of the property (see page 54). It is in the landlord's interest to control all of the restoration and not have numerous different contractors swarming around the building at the same time. From the tenant's standpoint, it may have had to do build-out once, but that is not what it is in the business to do.

As to the rent abatement, leases often provide that the rent commences again when the landlord completes its restoration work. This should certainly not be the case if the tenant has to restore its improvements or alterations, and it should not be the case, as well, if the tenant has to re-fixture the premises and install its equipment, merchandise, and other personal property. The tenant should be afforded a reasonable period of time to do so.

Leases sometimes give the landlord the right to terminate the lease if certain conditions exist, such as the length of time that will be required to restore, or the fact that all or substantially all of the (multi-tenant) building has been destroyed. They do not usually give the tenant the same right, except possibly close to the end of the term or if the restoration is not commenced when required in the lease or completed within some period—which the landlord will want to be an extended period. The landlord has a good reason for that: if the tenant has the right to terminate, the lender may not make the insurance proceeds available to restore and the landlord will have to refinance the property in order to do so (assuming the loan is pre-payable). New financing may not be readily available (it will be a construction loan), or the rate may be substantially higher than the rate with the existing lender (which may be why the lender is so eager to retain the proceeds).

Sometimes a lease form will provide that the landlord's right to terminate is triggered by the premises being untenantable (defined on page 56), which means that they may not be occupied. This is really unfair to the tenant since the premises may be untenantable for reasons other than material damage to the premises themselves. For example, there may be water damage in the premises because of a fire on an upper floor or because the elevators are unusable due to a fire and the tenant cannot access its upper-level space.

In that case, the landlord may terminate the lease because it wants to get more rent in an up market, not because of the damage. If untenantability is the standard, it should be tied to some substantial duration. A better standard for termination is that it would take a long specified time to restore or that the cost of restoration exceeds a specified number. If the landlord terminates and then restores the premises, perhaps the tenant should be afforded a right to lease the space again, on the same terms as before; that right will keep the landlord honest.

I have already discussed the inadvisability of conditioning the rent abatement on the tenant not having caused the fire (see page 56). Such a provision is not in the interest of any party except the insurance company, which does not then have to pay the proceeds of the rent insurance, which was paid for, directly or indirectly, by the tenant.

Condemnation

Properties are sometimes taken for some public or quasi-public purpose by a governmental agency or other entity (sometimes even a utility) having the power of eminent domain. For example, a property, or part of a property, may be taken for a road widening, for an airport expansion, to build a school, or for public transportation purposes. A municipality may want to change the grade of a street, and the result is to render the adjoining property unusable for its existing purpose. These are all "takings" or "condemnations," and the condemning body is obligated under the U.S. Constitution to pay "just compensation," commonly known as the "award." Every lease has a section dealing with condemnation, which usually favors the landlord, and the parties sometimes spend endless hours negotiating that section. Often that is a waste of time. Why? Because the likelihood of a taking in any given situation is remote. Sometimes the parties may be surprised and be subject to an unexpected condemnation, but to be realistic, a high-rise building in the central business district of a major city is not going to be condemned.

Consider a total taking, when the lease is terminated. In a ground lease situation, if the landlord owns the land and the tenant owns the building, at least during the term of the lease, each party has a measurable loss from the taking and can legitimately argue for a substantial portion of the condemnation award. In a long-term lease for a big-box store, the tenant has some argument to share in the award since it is losing the benefit of its bargain—and it may also have the economic clout to get something. In the more typical lease, however, the landlord is losing its property, and its lender is entitled to have its loan paid off. Although the tenant is certainly losing its leasehold estate (which is an interest in the property) and the benefit of its lease, which may be a rental rate below current market or a very favorable location, the tenant is not likely to be able to convince the landlord or its lender to share the award with it. The tenant may get moving expenses or the cost of any personal property taken (although it can probably remove and keep that property) as part of a separate award, or it may be able to squeeze out something for the unamortized value of expensive leasehold improvements or alterations (unlikely), but generally it will need a lot of bargaining clout to get much of a share of the landlord's award.

In the case of a taking of a part of the property, leases sometime tie termination of the lease to the percentage of the premises taken. That is inappropriate because the location of the portion of the premises taken, not the size of the taking, will probably dictate whether the space still has value to the tenant for the conduct of its business. A better standard is whether the premises can still be used for the same purpose and with substantially the same utility to the tenant as before the taking. In either case, if the lease is not terminated, the landlord will customarily agree to restore the balance of the premises (but not to spend more than the award) and to reduce the rent on some equitable basis.

Options and Other Special Rights of the Tenant

Let's turn to something with a bit more pizzazz than casualty losses and condemnation. While not usually in the landlord's lease form, options, rights of first refusal, and rights of first offer are often conditions to making a deal. There may be an option to extend the term (I prefer to refer to "extension" rather than to "renewal"), to lease additional premises, or even to purchase the property.[12] The tenant might insist on a right of first refusal to lease the adjoining space or to buy the building if the landlord decides to sell. The parties might agree that the landlord will offer to lease adjoining space or even to sell the building to the tenant before going to the market, which is commonly known as a right of first offer.

As I said before (see page 73), options are one-way streets. So are rights of first refusal and rights of first offer. Why is this so? It is because the landlord is restricted in its ability to deal with its property, but the tenant is not bound in any way other than to observe the terms of the right, and then only if it desires to exercise the right. For example, assume the tenant has an option to extend the term and really wants to continue its lease. It will make a determination whether the rent during the extension that is specified in the lease is a fair rental under the existing market conditions (each party's broker may be consulted for the information). If the specified rent is lower than the market, the tenant will exercise the option. If it is higher, the tenant will not exercise the option but will attempt to negotiate an extension at the then current market rate. Of course, the landlord may not really want to keep this tenant, either because it has not been a great tenant or because another tenant (who is possibly larger or has better credit) needs the space. In that case, the tenant may have to exercise the option, even at a higher-than-market rent in order to stay in the space. In either case, it is the tenant rather than the landlord that benefits. Similar logic applies to the other rights covered by this section of the book.

I have listed three rights at the beginning of this section. What are the differences?

Options

If the tenant has an option, it has been afforded a continuing irrevocable offer, either to extend the term, take additional space, buy the building, or whatever else is provided in the option language, in accordance with the predesignated terms specified in the lease. Even if the rent for the extended term is to be determined by some form of appraisal, the way the appraisal

---

12. There may be rights to terminate the lease or exclude portions of the premises. They are also options, but not customarily referred to as such.

is to be conducted is (or should be) set forth in the option provision in the lease. All that the tenant needs to do to accept the continuing offer is to exercise the option in the manner and within the time period specified in the option language.

An example might help. Assume that the tenant has an option to lease the adjoining space in an office building. In well-drafted language, the suite number and size of the space will be set out (and perhaps even a drawing to show the dimensions will be included), and the rent to be paid, any rent concessions, landlord construction, or tenant allowance will be specified. If the space is to be leased on a gross-lease basis with stops, the new base will be specified, if appropriate. The other terms of the original lease will be reviewed by the drafter and his or her counterpart to determine whether all the other terms of the original lease apply, or whether there is a need to include other provisions relating specifically to the option space. If the rent is to be based on "market," the relevant market will be defined (by geographic area and by quality of building) and the decision maker(s) (whether appraisers or brokers—I prefer brokers because they know the terms of deals in the relevant market) and the method of deciding will be included. (A fuller discussion of market rent starts on page 122.)

The method I like is for each party to choose a broker, each of whom is unrelated to either party. Each broker comes up with a rent. If the rent determined by the higher is within 10 percent of the lower, the designated rent is averaged. If the 10 percent formula does not work, the brokers select a third broker, who makes the decision. Because this method is expensive and time-consuming, and because the amount of the rent is not the only factor to be considered in determining "market," the parties do not usually resort to this (or any other method), but manage somehow to agree on the terms.

In the case of a market rent deal, the tenant might seek to have the right to revoke its exercise of the option if it is not satisfied with the rent, or there may be a way for the rent to be determined before the exercise of the option. That makes it even more of a one-way street. However, if the landlord reserves the right to terminate the option if it is not satisfied with the rent, it is not much of an option since the landlord has, in effect, the right to revoke the continuing offer described above.

Options specify a time period within which they must be exercised, or the occurrence of an event that triggers the option. An option to extend may have to be exercised six months or more before the end of the term. The length of time is often heavily negotiated since the tenant wants to have as short a period as possible so it can evaluate its business and needs based on conditions the tenant anticipates will exist in the future. The landlord, however, wants a long period so it has time to lease the option space (or sell the building) before the tenant's lease expires. Of course, larger spaces, or spaces with specialized uses, take longer to lease and the landlord will want even longer periods in those situations. If the rent or price is to be market determined, the parties will usually agree that the option cannot be exercised before a certain date, so that the consideration will actually reflect the then-market conditions. Generally speaking, the option must be exercised with the time specified, or the exercise is not effective. For that reason, it is important that the parties review the notice section of the lease to determine whether notices are effective when sent or when received, since a notice may be sent before the time to exercise expires, but received after (remember I mentioned that even notice provisions have economic effect). Many leases provide that "time is of the essence" and in some jurisdictions, unless that language is included, courts will be lenient if the exercise date is missed and the right is exercised somewhat late. In other jurisdictions, that is not an issue. The right must be exercised on time.

Rights of First Refusal

If a tenant has a right of first refusal, such as to lease adjoining space, the landlord must go to the market and try to lease the space to another party. When the landlord finds that third party, it must negotiate the terms of the lease relative to that space—whether a letter of intent will do or whether the parties must actually negotiate the lease is a matter to be handled in the drafting. When the terms are agreed upon, the landlord goes to the tenant, discloses the terms of the other deal and the tenant has some period of time, usually a short period because the other party will not wait forever, to lease the space on the same terms and conditions. The same procedure applies in the case of a right of first refusal to buy or even to lease the same space at the expiration of the term. What happens if the landlord is unable to find the "other party" before the lease expires will have to be dealt with in the negotiations.

It sounds like a good idea; after all, what could be a fairer test of value and of market terms than what a third party is willing to agree to?

Actually, I despise rights of first refusal and will bend every effort to prevent my client from agreeing to them. Why?

1. It is unfair to the third party. If the third party knew in advance that it was being used to determine value and might not get the deal it bargained for, it would not be willing to spend the time—and more importantly the money—to negotiate the deal (particularly if it had to finalize the document before the "offer" was submitted to the tenant). Of course, the landlord could tell the third party about the right of first refusal and hope that the third party wants the space so badly that it is willing to take the risk, but the chances are that the third party would simply walk away. Would you not advise your client to do so?

2. It is unfair to the landlord. The landlord, too, has to go through the time and expense of negotiating the other deal. Certainly the effort will not be wasted, because one or the other party will be bound, but still, the landlord has the unpleasant choice of telling the third party that there is a right of first refusal and possibly watching the third party disappear, or fail to disclose and be in what is certainly an unethical position. If the landlord uses a broker to market the space to third parties, then the broker is the party confronted with the dilemma of disclosing or not disclosing, plus a further dilemma of having to follow the landlord's decision not to disclose or walking away from the deal.

3. The landlord has another issue. It may have agreed with the tenant's broker to pay a full commission on the expansion, purchase, or whatever was the subject matter of the right of first refusal, and the broker representing the third party may claim a commission, even if the right is exercised, on the ground that he was actually the procuring cause of the exercise of the right, by bringing to the table the third party who was ready, willing, and able to do the deal.

4. It is not such a great thing for tenants either. The main problem is that the time for the tenant to exercise the right is usually pretty

short—five to seven days at most. That is because the landlord cannot expect the third party to wait around, whether it knows about the right or not. This puts a lot of pressure on the tenant to make a decision very quickly, and particularly in big companies, that is hard to accomplish. The more the tenant presses for a longer time to decide, the more unfair the right becomes for the landlord and the third party.

Needless to say, even when all the problems with rights of first refusal are described, parties still insist on them, particularly tenants. Still, there is an alternative, which I suggest, that will satisfy the tenant, and that is the right of first offer.

Rights of First Offer

In granting a right of first offer, the landlord agrees that before going to market to lease the adjoining space, or sell the building, or whatever is the subject matter of the right, it will offer it to the tenant. That offer will set forth the consideration to be paid by the tenant, which the landlord agrees will be based on a good faith estimate of the true value, and the tenant will have a period of time, usually longer than under the right of first refusal, to accept the landlord's offer. And it may afford the parties an opportunity to negotiate a deal after the offer is made to the tenant without the pressure of a third-party offer.

Assume, however, that the following negotiation occurs in connection with a right of first offer to lease the adjoining space. "Okay," says the tenant, "but what if the rent you quoted is not really the market rent and you and I cannot negotiate an acceptable rent? I trust you, but what if you sell the building and your successor is not so honorable?" (The hypothetical evil successor is a very handy foil in lease negotiations.)

This is a very legitimate concern with rights of first offer, so Steve Podolsky and I created a new form.

Right of First Offer with a Back-End Right of First Refusal

This approach combines the right of first offer with a means to determine value if the parties are unable to agree. It works like this: The landlord specifies a price or rent, as the case may be, and the tenant may accept that amount or make a counteroffer. If the tenant makes a counteroffer, the parties have a certain length of time to agree, but if they are unable to do so, the landlord goes to the market and gets an offer from a disinterested third party, just as in the case of the right of first refusal. Then, if the landlord is willing to accept an offer or to make an offer to a third party for a price or rent that is less than the greater of 95 percent (or another specified percentage) of the offer price or rent specified by the landlord and the counteroffer price or rent offered by the tenant, the tenant has the right to lease or purchase the property at the price offered by the third party that was acceptable to the landlord.

That is a bit complicated, so an example might be helpful. Assume that the right of first offer relates to the purchase of the property of which the premises are a part. Let's say that the landlord makes a "first offer" to sell the property to the tenant for $10 million. The tenant's highest counteroffer is $9.3 million and the parties cannot agree. The landlord goes to the market and gets a $9.5 million offer from a third party. The landlord can then sell the property to the third party; the price is 95 percent of the landlord's offer. If the third party offer is $9.49 million, however, the tenant has the right to match that offer and buy the property because the price is less than 95 percent of the landlord's offer. If the tenant's offer was $9.6 million, and the third-party offer, which the landlord desired to accept, is $9.55 million, that was less than the tenant's counteroffer, and the landlord would be obligated to reoffer the property to the tenant for $9.55 million. Complicated? Sure!

The point is not necessarily that the parties will use these formulas to determine the price or the rent. The point is that, because the parties will be concerned about the outcome and the cost and delay of getting to that outcome, they will communicate even before the first offer is made by the landlord and agree on a price or rent, or a simple formula for determining it. The parties may fight over the language in the lease, but if the contemplated situation arises, the parties will probably figure out a way to resolve the issues without following the procedures fought over.

Accessibility

The Americans with Disabilities Act of 1990 (ADA)—and regulations and guidelines promulgated under it, as they may be amended and supplemented from time to time—is federal law pertaining to accessibility for people with disabilities.

Title III of ADA establishes requirements pertaining to business operations, accessibility, and barrier removal, and those requirements may be unclear, and may or may not apply to the various premises, buildings, or the properties depending on, among other things, whether (a) the tenant's business operations are deemed a "place of public accommodation" or a "commercial facility," (b) compliance with such requirements is "readily achievable" or "technically infeasible," and (c) a given condition or alteration affects a "primary function area" or triggers "path of travel" requirements.

The ADA has a specific list of what is deemed a place of public accommodation, as follows:

A. an inn, hotel, motel, or other place of lodging, except for an establishment located within a building that contains not more than five rooms for rent or hire and that is actually occupied by the proprietor of such establishment as the residence of such proprietor;

B. a restaurant, bar, or other establishment serving food or drink;

C. a motion picture house, theater, concert hall, stadium, or other place of exhibition or entertainment;

D. an auditorium, convention center, lecture hall, or other place of public gathering;

E. a bakery, grocery store, clothing store, hardware store, shopping center, or other sales or rental establishment;

F. a laundromat, dry-cleaner, bank, barbershop, beauty shop, travel service, shoe repair service, funeral parlor, gas station, office of an accountant or lawyer, pharmacy, insurance office, professional office of a health care provider, hospital, or other service establishment;

G. a terminal, depot, or other station used for specified public transportation;

H. a museum, library, gallery, or other place of public display or collection;

   I. a park, zoo, amusement park, or other place of recreation;

   J. a nursery, elementary, secondary, undergraduate, or postgraduate private school, or other place of education;

   K. a day care center, senior citizen center, homeless shelter, food bank, adoption agency, or other social service center establishment; and

   L. a gymnasium, health spa, bowling alley, golf course, or other place of exercise or recreation.

Other businesses, such as warehouses or offices not listed above, are categorized as "commercial facilities." Under ADA, the standard for accessibility for places of public accommodation is much greater than for commercial facilities. This is a highly technical area of the law, and it is not appropriate to delve into it too much here, but brokers should be aware of the issues and, if appropriate, seek counsel from lawyers or architects with expertise in this area. They should also be aware that many states and local governments have accessibility requirements that may or may not exceed the national standard.

The main accessibility issue for brokers is the allocation of responsibility for compliance. This is, of course, a matter of negotiation based on market conditions and the respective situations of the parties.

Covenant of Quiet Enjoyment

Oddly, the covenant of quiet enjoyment has nothing to do with noise. It has to do with title.

The law implies a covenant of quiet enjoyment in every lease—an agreement by the landlord that the tenant's use and occupancy of the premises will not be disturbed by other claimants. In other words, if the landlord did not really own the property when it signed the lease and put the tenant in possession of the premises, and the tenant is evicted by the real owner or the real owner demands an exorbitant increase in rent, that would constitute a breach of the covenant, which gives rise to a cause of action against the landlord—which is to say, a reason the landlord might be required by a court to pay damages to the tenant. Likewise, if the landlord mortgages the premises and as a result of a foreclosure the tenant is evicted, the tenant could seek damages from the landlord.

Most leases contain a "Covenant of Quiet Enjoyment" section, but if you review it, you will find that it is not very broad. In fact, it is less broad than the implied covenant. For example, the section might read: "So long as no Event of Default of Tenant has occurred, Tenant's quiet and peaceable enjoyment of the Leased Premises shall not be disturbed or interfered with by Landlord or by any person claiming by, through or under Landlord."

As you can see, this language does nothing to protect the tenant against a claimant with a prior right to the premises.

The covenant of quiet enjoyment, while it is in every lease and is somewhat interesting to consider, no longer has the same impact as it did formerly. In most commercial leases these days, the landlord is an entity that owns nothing other than the property, all or a portion of which is leased to the tenant. It is a corporation or a limited liability company or even a trust, and probably is a single-purpose entity. If the tenancy is interfered with by a prior claimant or by the landlord's lender and, as a result, the landlord loses the property, recourse against the landlord is useless since the particular landlord has nothing left and the tenant does not have any right to recourse against the owners of the entity because they have been insulated from personal liability.

So how does the tenant protect itself? It can seek a guaranty from the owners of the landlord entity—but don't hold your breath. It can seek a non-disturbance agreement (discussed in detail starting on page 41) from the lender (or ground lessor, if there is one), but a small tenant might not get one, or it can buy title insurance insuring its leasehold estate (since a lease creates an interest in the real estate). Title insurance is certainly a necessity for ground leases or for other long-term leases that are critical for the tenant, but it involves expense and delay. Further, it only protects the tenant against prior claimants and not against any future foreclosure or other claim arising thereafter. If there is to be title insurance for the tenant, the lease should be conditioned on the tenant's obtaining it.

Enough said about this provision. Let's move on to something more interesting.

Defaults and Remedies

Tenant's Defaults and Landlord's Remedies

Although many lease forms list numerous events as tenant defaults or events of default, the principal concerns of the landlord are the payment of monthly rent, the payment of additional rent, the adherence of the tenant to carry the insurance required of it under the lease, and the performance of the other specified obligations of the tenant under the lease. The lease may also deal with insolvency events by the tenant and may even seek to make repeated defaults an "event of default" that could trigger the landlord's remedies.

I have referred to defaults and events of default. Leases try to deal with the fact that if, for example, the tenant does not pay its rent by the first of the month, if required to do so under the lease, it is in default or breach, but if the lease provides that the tenant has a period of time thereafter, or after notice, to cure the failure to pay, the landlord does not have any remedies until it has given the notice, if required, and the time to cure has elapsed. Leases often refer to the failure to pay as a "default" and the failure to pay after the time to cure as a "Default" or an "Event of Default." In that way, these have become defined terms.

Payment of rent is, of course, critical to the landlord. Without prompt payment, the landlord might default under its mortgage or be unable to meet its other obligations, or even be able to make distributions to its investors. Still, most leases give the tenant a cure period, such as five days. Tenants often argue for longer cure periods. Many leases give a cure period, but do not tie it to the giving of notice. That, to me, is unfair. It severely penalizes the tenant who does not know that its check, which may have been sent on time, has not arrived. Landlords sometimes agree to give notice one or two times a year, after which the tenant may be at risk. It is not illogical, although it is not such a great burden on landlords to give a notice, but my lease forms just provide for five days after notice. On the other hand, my lease form contains a repeated default clause.

Many leases provide that the failure to pay the rent on time causes interest to be payable at a default rate. The default rate may be a set amount or an amount tied to some external rate, such as the prime rate as published in the *Wall Street Journal* or some other business publication. Leases used to provide for a default rate of 7 percent per annum, but in the early 1980s, prime rate rose to over 20 percent, so the default rate was a bargain. As this is being written, prime is extremely low, so 7 percent would be tantamount to a penalty rate. Usually when the prime rate is referred to, the default rate is prime plus some additional percentage, such as prime plus 4 percent, changing as prime changes. The additional percentage is often the subject of negotiation.

Some leases may provide for a late fee. The landlord must not be too greedy, because a very substantial late fee may be deemed to be a penalty and unenforceable. A late fee of 5 percent of the delinquent payment is pretty common, but other amounts are often negotiated. Tenants often seek a grace period before these charges kick in, and sometimes those are granted, but they, too, may be limited to a specified number in a year. This is a touchy subject. Hard as it may be to believe, at a time of recession or slow economic growth, but with high inflation and high interest rates, many large companies deliberately paid their rents late so they would have the use of the money or be able to earn interest on it during the grace period. Landlords who know that history want to make certain it does not repeat itself.

As to other obligations of the tenant, a cure period of 30 days is pretty common. Exceptions might be the cure period for keeping the insurance in effect, or for providing documents required for the landlord to obtain its financing, or for dealing with emergency situations, which might be considerably shorter. As to nonpayment defaults that cannot with due diligence be cured within 30 days, the tenant is (or should be) allowed additional time to cure, provided it commenced promptly and proceeds diligently to cure. I do not understand why a time limit (such as "not to exceed 60 days") is sometimes inserted. Is the landlord interested in having the problem cured or in having a lawsuit against the tenant? Some cures, such as roof replacement, may not be feasible during the winter.

The remedies available for uncured Defaults or Events of Default vary from jurisdiction to jurisdiction, so it is impossible to enumerate them here. In Illinois, the landlord may simply sue for the rent, leaving the tenant in possession of the premises and bound to perform all of its obligations under its lease. On the other hand, the landlord may terminate the tenant's right to possession of the premises without terminating the lease and continue to collect the rent unless the premises are relet (and then still collect any shortfall). And the landlord may, in the alternative, terminate the lease and collect damages, being the difference between the rent specified in the lease and the fair rental value of the premises, each for the balance of the term (but subject to a discount rate). Illinois also provides for a statutory duty to mitigate damages, which I know does not exist in all states. Brokers should become aware of the remedies permitted and generally provided for in leases pertaining to their states.

Most leases also provide that the landlord has the right to cure the tenant's default and the cost becomes additional rent due from the tenant to the landlord, with interest at some specified default rate. The tenant will, of course, be concerned about the cost, and will seek to limit the expenditure to a "reasonable cost" standard. On the other hand, the landlord does not want to have to litigate the reasonableness of the cost, and may seek to make it "actual cost," perhaps with a good faith standard (which might involve the landlord in litigation anyway).

Many leases provide very extensive and specific remedies in the event of a bankruptcy. Because the bankruptcy court will determine remedies, irrespective of the provisions of the lease, it is my view that those provisions may safely be ignored, especially by brokers.

Landlord's Defaults and Tenant's Remedies

Most leases are silent on the subject of the tenant's remedies for the landlord's defaults. This is not surprising because most leases are written, initially at least, by landlords. Most states adhere to the rule that, unlike in contracts generally, if the landlord defaults, the tenant does not have the right to terminate the lease except in the case of "constructive eviction," which occurs when the landlord's default permanently prevents the tenant from operating in the premises. In that regard, the courts follow an ancient rule in real estate lease cases that the obligations agreed to by the tenant (referred to as "independent covenants") are independent of the landlord's obligations and that the tenant's remedy, in the absence of express language in the lease, is to sue the landlord for damages.

Some tenants, especially major tenants with a lot of clout, get a right to cure the landlord's default. The way it usually works is that if the landlord does not cure within 30 days (shorter in an emergency), the tenant has the right to cure at the landlord's expense. When representing a landlord, I usually seek an additional five-day notice before the tenant begins to cure because the landlord may have contracted for the cure, and the landlord does not want the tenant to do so and cause the landlord to have to pay twice. Many, but not all, leases that include the tenant's right to cure (sometimes referred to as "self-help") provide that if the landlord does not pay the cost of the cure within a specified period, the tenant has the right to deduct the cost from rent thereafter payable. The landlord may seek to limit the deduction right to base rent (so it has the funds to pay taxes and other pass-through items), or even to a percentage of base rent (so the landlord has the funds to pay its debt service). As in the case of the landlord curing the tenant's default, the landlord will want to ensure that the tenant's cost of curing is controlled.

If the landlord has several tenants on the property that desire self-help remedies, it must be very careful. The last thing the landlord wants is for more than one tenant to contract for snow removal or roof repair. Once the landlord has granted a tenant such a remedy as to common areas, it should advise subsequent tenants to work with the tenant who already has the right to cure.

Security Deposits

The irony of security deposits is that the landlord always needs the most from the tenant that can least afford to pay one. Sometimes the problem is solved by having principals of the tenant post the security, especially if the security deposit is in the form of a letter of credit (discussed on page 98).

Actually, the landlord would like a security deposit from each tenant, even the ones with excellent credit. Why? Because many tenants, even ones with great credit, damage premises or surrender them other than in the condition required in the lease. Also, as we learned during the recession of 2008, many companies we thought were strong turned out not to be. Who would ever have thought that a security deposit from General Motors Corporation would really be needed?

Some landlords typically ask for a security deposit based on one, two, or three months' rent. That, in my judgment, is pretty shortsighted. The security deposit should actually be determined based on the amount of the landlord's risk. Obviously, the landlord should seek a more substantial security deposit from a weak tenant than a strong one. It is not unusual, in the case of a substantial security deposit, to provide for its reduction from time to time as the risk to the landlord decreases, provided the tenant is not in default.

In addition, I have already discussed the situation in which the landlord did special construction for a tenant and needed assurance that the funds were available if that special construction had to be removed to make the premises usable by a subsequent tenant (see pages 19-20). The landlord may be making a large landlord contribution toward the tenant's improvements and want to know it can recover the unamortized portion of that expense (as well as its brokers' commissions) if the tenant defaults during the term.

Sometimes landlords accept a guaranty instead of a security deposit or reduce the amount of the security deposit based on a guaranty. I will discuss guaranties below (see page 101).

The security deposit section should provide, as it typically does, that the landlord can apply all or a portion of the security deposit to cure defaults. Some sections also provide that the security deposit may be applied to "damages," which makes the landlord, rather than a court, the judge of the amount of damages; when representing a tenant, I argue that such a provision is inappropriate. The section customarily goes on to require the tenant to restore the security deposit to its prior amount in the event of an application. The section may permit commingling of the security deposit with the landlord's other funds and not provide for interest, both of which provisions may be problematic for tenants and, in some states, may not even be permitted. In addition, the section should specify the length of time after the lease expires when the security deposit is to be returned.

It is an open secret, but not necessarily known to tenants, that the real reason the landlord wants a security deposit from every tenant is because it needs the funds to pay the security deposit back to the prior tenant, or to pay the commission or to pay for construction. That being the case, the right to commingle could be a problem when it comes to getting the security deposit back when the lease expires. There is a further issue of what right the tenant has in commingled funds if the landlord is in bankruptcy.

Letters of Credit

Oddly enough, except for small security deposits, the landlord and the tenant both have advantages from having the security deposit held in the form of a letter of credit. Although the landlord will not be able to use the security deposit for other purposes (which is not very legitimate anyway), the letter of credit gives the landlord a very substantial advantage: if it holds a letter of credit and the tenant goes into bankruptcy, the landlord may draw on the letter of credit and apply the funds as provided in the security deposit section. The thing to be mindful of is that, for a period of time after the filing of a bankruptcy, all parties dealing with the bankrupt parties are subject to an automatic stay, which prevents them from doing any act affecting the bankrupt party. They may not even give a notice of default to the bankrupt party, even if the bankrupt party is actually in default. That is why the landlord may not agree to give a notice of default to the tenant before drawing on the letter of credit, because it may not be permitted to give that notice and thus is prohibited by the terms of the lease from drawing on the letter of credit until the automatic stay is lifted and the notice may be given, thus losing a great advantage. Since the bank issuing the letter of credit, and not the tenant, is the debtor under that letter of credit, the automatic stay does not prevent the landlord from drawing on the letter of credit and using it as provided in the lease. It is the bank that is prohibited from using the security posted by the tenant to secure the issuance of the letter of credit, at least until the automatic stay is lifted. If the tenant is concerned about the lack of notice before the draw, a compromise might be for the landlord to be obligated to give the notice unless it is prevented from doing so by an automatic stay, in which case the notice would not be required.

An important issue for the landlord is that the bank issuing the letter of credit is sound financially. If the issuing bank becomes insolvent, neither the FDIC nor a bank acquiring the assets of the insolvent bank can be required to honor the letter of credit. Another important issue is to ensure that the letter of credit is in effect as long as the security deposit is to be made in accordance with the lease. A way of assuring that is to require an "evergreen" letter of credit, which renews automatically unless the issuing bank gives advance notice that it will not be renewed, in which case the language of the lease, as well as the letter of credit, should permit the landlord to draw on the letter of credit before it actually expires.

The landlord will want to make certain that the security deposit can be held for a sufficient period after the lease expires to enable the landlord to use the proceeds to make repairs required by the tenant's acts or omissions or to pay for the removal of property abandoned by the tenant. In addition, if rent must be returned to a trustee or debtor in possession because it is deemed a preference under the bankruptcy code, the landlord needs to hold the security deposit (or have the letter of credit to continue in effect) so it can recapture that returned rent from the security deposit (or the proceeds of the letter of credit). Since the period within which a preference repayment may be required under the bankruptcy code is, at this writing, 90 days, the return of the security deposit should occur 100 days after the lease expires (giving the landlord a 10-day grace period). Since that is a long period for the landlord to hold the security deposit, the tenant may request that the lease provide that if the tenant establishes that the conditions that allow a preference do not exist, the security deposit will be returned within 30 days. That is a reasonable request.

Note that the tenant will be required to give security to the bank in order for the bank to issue the letter of credit, and will have to pay a fee to the bank for that letter. Still, the advantage for the tenant is the assurance that the letter of credit will expire around the end of the term and it will not have to chase a landlord that may be insolvent for the return of its cash security deposit.

Brokers representing landlords that require letters of credit should be aware that banks charge the beneficiary of the letter of credit (i.e., the landlord) a substantial amount (such as .25 percent of the amount of the letter of credit, with a hefty minimum) if the letter of credit is transferred to another beneficiary, as would occur if the property is sold. If the landlord, in negotiating the lease, states that it will pay no more than, say, $100 for a transfer, this puts the onus on the tenant to negotiate a reduced fee with its bank. It should be clear in the negotiations that any fee in excess of the amount specified in the lease will have to be paid by the tenant. That often results in some flexibility by the issuing bank, since it is a charge made with little or no corresponding cost to the bank.

Other Noncash Security Deposits

On occasion, I have seen tenants ask that the security deposit be in the form of a bond, or that the tenant be allowed to deposit securities instead of cash. Neither of these is a good idea.

Perhaps the tenant will not have to deposit security with the bonding company as it would with a bank, but the cost of the bond will be a lot more than the cost of a letter of credit. The landlord should have a serious problem with the bond too, because unlike the letter of credit, which must be paid within 24 or 48 hours after a draw, the bonding company is under no compulsion to pay promptly, and it may even take a lawsuit to get paid, especially if the tenant is insolvent.

The problem with the posting of securities, other than the risk of decline in value, is that it takes a great deal of documentation to accomplish, so that both parties are protected.

Guaranties

A security deposit is better for the landlord than a guaranty, provided that it is sufficient in amount to assure performance of the lease obligations of the tenant. Still, there are numerous reasons for a landlord to insist on a guaranty, whether or not a security deposit is provided. First, it gives the landlord another bite at the apple if for some reason the tenant does not or cannot perform. Second, unless it is specifically limited, it guarantees all the obligations under the lease. Third, the landlord may, in a properly drafted guaranty, proceed against the guarantor even if the tenant is in bankruptcy.

I discussed above the situation in which a tenant is a subsidiary of another company and does not have its own financial statement (see page 46). The parent company will almost always be in a better financial position than the subsidiary, so its guaranty will fill the gap in credit. In another situation, the tenant may be a start-up with no established credit. If the principal of the tenant, either an individual, a group of individuals, or another company, does have a decent financial statement, that party or parties may be asked to sign a guaranty to ensure performance.

Just what does a guaranty provide? If it is a payment and performance guaranty, as is typically used, the guarantor will undertake to make all payments and perform all the obligations of the tenant. The landlord will generally insist that the guaranty be primary, which is to say that the landlord is not required to exhaust its remedies against the tenant before proceeding against the guarantor. The guarantor will agree to pay all the costs of enforcing the guaranty and will agree that, if the tenant pays rent but the landlord must pay that rent over to a bankruptcy trustee (because the payment was a preference), the guarantor will reimburse the landlord.

The guaranty will generally require that the guarantor waive the right to any notice of default. This certainly appears unfair. However, the reason is that, since guaranties are very strictly construed to protect the guarantor, there is a risk to the landlord that if it misses giving a notice, the entire guaranty may become unenforceable. A compromise position on that issue might be to provide that if the notice is missed, the guarantor cannot collect as to that default, but the guaranty remains in effect as to other defaults to which notice is given. I have used that language and I hope it is enforceable, but I have never seen it litigated.

The guaranty will also generally require the guarantor to waive any other defenses it might have, but I have gotten landlords to limit the waiver to what is called "suretyship defenses," which are defenses pertaining to guaranties only.

If one entity guaranties the obligations of another, there is always an issue as to whether there is a sufficient relationship between the parties because, unless there is such a relationship, or the guarantor receives consideration for giving the guaranty, the guarantor may have a defense against an action seeking to collect on the guaranty. The guaranty may be "ultra vires," or beyond the corporate or other legal power of the guarantor.

I have been involved in situations where an American subsidiary of a major foreign entity negotiates a lease in the United States and, because the American subsidiary does not have adequate credit, the guaranty of the foreign entity is required. That presents some serious and special problems.

If the guarantor is a company incorporated or organized in the United States, it can be sued somewhere in the United States, either in its principal place of business, in the state of its incorporation or organization, or in some state (including the one where the premises are located) where it is doing business. If the landlord is in a state other than the guarantor's, and the amount at issue exceeds the specified statutory limit, the action may be brought in the federal district court where either the plaintiff or the defendant resides. In any case, if a judgment is obtained, it is entitled to "full faith and credit," which means that, once the judgment is registered in other states, it is readily enforceable against assets of the guarantor located in those states.

If, on the other hand, the guarantor is incorporated in a foreign country, the situation is much more complicated. First, there is a question as to whether the foreign guarantor must be sued in its own country, which would be exceedingly inconvenient or, on the other hand, it can be sued where the property is located. The guaranty should specify that the guarantor agrees that it may be sued in a court where the property is located. Second, there is a concern as to how the guarantor may be brought into that court. Usually a case is commenced by the filing of a complaint, after which the clerk of the court issues a summons, which is served by the sheriff or other official either directly at the office of the defendant or of a company or individual named as the registered agent for the defendant. Thus the foreign guarantor should designate a party in the area where the agreed-to court is located, to accept service of a summons on behalf of the guarantor. If it or its American subsidiary has no office in that state, it may designate the secretary of state of that state to accept that service. Third, the guaranty should specify that the law of the state where the premises are located is the governing law relative to the guaranty; the parties do not want the law of the foreign country to control.

Finally, assuming a judgment is entered against the guarantor where the property is located, how is it to be collected when the guarantor's assets are in a foreign country? That is a tricky question because chances are neither the lawyer representing the landlord nor a local counsel representing the tenant is familiar with the law of that country. What I generally do is request that the guarantor deliver a legal opinion from an attorney licensed in the foreign country that states that the guaranty is duly executed and delivered and is binding on the guarantor, and that a judgment obtained in the court in the United States is enforceable in the foreign country without having to retry the factual issues in the case. I have received such opinions, and some of them have been qualified, which provided important information. For example, I received an opinion from a German lawyer that the judgment was enforceable if no pretrial discovery was conducted. Discovery was (and perhaps still is) against public policy in Germany. That was extremely important to know because it would govern how litigation against the guarantor was conducted in the United States, discovery being very routine here.

Of course, the guaranty may come from an individual or group of individuals, and not an entity. The issues with foreign individuals are the same as with entities. I just want to note that if the principal asset of an individual guarantor is his or her home, the landlord may have great hesitation to enforce the guaranty and put the guarantor and his or her family on the street. In fact, depending on how the home is owned, that remedy might not even be available.

I have seen tenants offer a "payment guaranty," limiting the landlord's remedy to collect from the guarantor only if the landlord has exhausted its remedies against the tenant (in court) and has been unable to collect from the tenant. That could involve the landlord in extensive litigation against a defaulting tenant (including appeals and actions to collect), which makes the guaranty somewhat useless. Such a guaranty should at least provide that the guarantor will pay the legal fees of the landlord in the litigation against the tenant.

Other Security

Many landlords seek a security interest in their tenants' personal property. In some states statutory law provides such security interests, unless they are expressly waived by the landlord. No such law applies in my state of Illinois, but leases often require that security. If it is provided for in the lease, the landlord will have to "perfect" the security interest by filing a financing statement as required by the Uniform Commercial Code in effect in that state or it may be subject to the rights of later creditors who do take a security interest and file, or to bona fide purchasers of the personal property for value without notice of the security interest. Tenants typically object to granting security interests in their personal property because that can really affect its ability to do business with that property. Of course a retailer or wholesaler does not want to pledge its merchandise because that would complicate its sale. Even pledging (which is a shorthand way of referring to the granting of a security interest) its furniture, furnishings, and equipment can hurt it, especially if it wants to borrow from a bank or other lending institution based on the value of that property. A very serious problem could arise if the pledge includes property such as computer software and computer programs developed by the tenant; if the landlord realizes on that security, it could just ruin the tenant's ability to do business.

As I mentioned, tenants sometimes borrow money from third parties and, to secure that loan, grant a security interest in personal property, including property located in the premises. The lender will often require a waiver from the landlord of any rights the landlord has or may obtain in the pledged property. The landlord may object to certain provisions in the waiver document, or may not want to waive at all. It is wise for brokers to address this issue during the lease negotiations. Some landlords' lawyers have a form of landlord's waiver, which has been, with some modifications, accepted by lenders in the past and which can be attached as an exhibit to the lease. I do.

Some states, including Illinois, have a statute that permits landlords to "distrain for rent." This means that, even before a judgment, the landlord can seize property of the tenant anywhere in the county to pay money claimed to be owed to the landlord. The landlord typically enters the premises, even if it has to break the lock, takes an inventory of what is located there and padlocks the door. The landlord must then file an action called a "distraint for rent," attaching the inventory to the complaint filed with the court. The landlord cannot seize property in which third parties have an interest, such as other lenders, but that can be worked out after the seizure. This course is pretty dangerous for landlords because tenants often complain that the landlord stole their property. My former partner joked that one must enter with three men of the cloth to act as witnesses that nothing was taken. This is not a common event, but it is still wise for a broker representing a tenant in a state with such a remedy to request that the lease provide that the right to distrain is waived.

Environmental Issues

Environmental problems may arise in any of the leasing situations, although they are most concerning to landlords and tenants in the case of industrial/warehouse lease situations, because the chemicals used in a manufacturing process or stored in warehouses may, if not used or stored in accordance with environmental laws, create substantial liability for both parties. A medical facility may generate unhealthy hazardous materials. Even a retail facility may be problematic, especially if it is selling home maintenance and repair items, or if it is an automobile dealership with a service center. Certainly gas stations have been prime polluters.

From the tenant's point of view, it is concerned that it may be moving into a facility whose environmental history is problematic. The landlord may not know what its property was used for before and certainly the tenant may have no better information. Of course, the landlord may have an environmental assessment (unless it has owned the property since before the passage of environmental legislation[13] and has not refinanced since that time), but that assessment may not be complete or accurate. Still, from the tenant's point of view, the landlord should assume the risk of liability arising from the environmental condition of the property existing at the time the lease is entered into. What is generally negotiated is that the landlord is responsible for remediation (except in ground lease and certain net lease situations, where the tenant must perform environmental testing as a condition of going forward with the lease, or the lease is be totally "as is, where is," and the environmental liability is expressly placed on the tenant). The lease may even contain an indemnity from the landlord for other related liabilities, but landlords strenuously contest that.

---

13. The Comprehensive Environmental Response, Compensation and Liability Act (referred to as CERCLA) was passed in 1980.

In most other lease situations, the tenant makes certain agreements about not using hazardous materials; if it does so, it is obligated to comply with good management practices and certainly to comply with applicable environmental laws and ordinances. It may have to indemnify the landlord for damages resulting from liability caused by the tenant's violation of such laws, but the tenant is generally only liable for what it causes. Even then, however, there is a wrinkle. What if hazardous materials then exist in the ground, but not in sufficient quantity or concentration to constitute a violation of law? Along comes the tenant who adds to the hazardous materials. The amount added is not, in itself, enough to constitute a violation, but because it is contributing to what already existed, a violation is created. Some landlords provide that such a contribution causing a violation where none existed before imposes the duty on the tenant to remediate.

Estoppel Certificates and SNDAs

What is an estoppel certificate, and why is it grouped in this discussion with something referred to as an SNDA?

Estoppel Certificates

The legal definition of "estop" is to stop, bar, or impede. When a party signs an estoppel certificate, it is barred from denying the accuracy of the matters stated in that certificate. Nearly all leases require the tenant to provide a signed estoppel certificate on the landlord's request. Sometimes a form of estoppel is attached to the lease, although a lender or buyer may request certifications in addition to the ones referred to in the lease or attached as an exhibit.

Why would a landlord require an estoppel certificate? If the landlord is closing a new mortgage on the property within which the premises are located, the lender will want to make certain that the information the landlord/borrower has provided about the leases is accurate and that there are no claims against the landlord which may adversely affect the value of its collateral or create a possible claim against the lender if it forecloses. Likewise, a prospective buyer will want the same certainty before it closes the purchase. Note that a tenant mortgaging its interest in the property (its leasehold estate) or assigning its lease, possibly in connection with the sale of its business, will want the right to require the landlord to issue its own estoppel certificate to confirm the truth of matters pertaining to the tenant's right to the interest being mortgaged or sold.

Bear in mind that if the estoppel certificate is addressed to the landlord as well as to the lender or prospective purchaser, the landlord may have the right to rely on it even if the facts stated are inaccurate.

Unfortunately, the broker will probably not be consulted when the tenant or landlord is asked to sign an estoppel certificate. Therefore it is incumbent on the broker (and the attorney for the client) to make certain, at the time the lease is entered into, that the client understands the importance of checking the accuracy of each statement when an estoppel is requested, because an inaccurate statement will be binding on the client. The client should feel free to revise the delivered document to make it accurate.

A typical estoppel requested from a tenant will seek the following confirmations (about which I will comment in italics):

1. Tenant is in full and complete possession of the premises demised under the lease, such possession having been delivered by the landlord pursuant to the lease and having been accepted by the tenant. The improvements to the premises that the landlord is required to furnish under the lease have been completed in all respects to the satisfaction of the tenant, and the premises are open for the use of the tenant, its customers, employees, and invitees. *If work to be performed by the landlord has not been completed or is not satisfactory, the defects should be itemized, and if the tenant is not certain of all the defects, it should state that fact or that the defects are only the ones that have been* discovered *at the time of the delivery of the estoppel. If the premises are not open for business, that should be stated.*

2. All contributions required to be paid by the landlord to the tenant in connection with improvements to the premises have been paid in full. *This one is very important, because if this is not true but that is not disclosed, the tenant will not have the right to collect from the lender (after foreclosure) or from the buyer.*

3. All duties or obligations of the landlord required under the lease that were an inducement to the tenant to enter into the lease have been fully performed. *The comment to item 2 applies here too.*

4. The lease is in full force and effect. No default exists on the part of the landlord or the tenant under the lease, nor does any circumstance currently exist that, but for the giving of notice or the passage of time, or both, would be such a default. *This is a trap. Generally the tenant does not know if the landlord has actually performed all of its obligations, so it should qualify this statement "to its knowledge."* The lease constitutes the entire rental agreement between the landlord and the tenant with respect to the premises and has not been amended, modified, or supplemented, except as attached hereto. *All amendments should be attached or referred to.* There are no oral agreements between the landlord and the tenant with respect to the premises. *Disclose any.* A true and correct copy of the lease (including all amendments thereto) is attached to this certificate *(this can be a nuisance—a reference to the lease should suffice, especially if there are many exhibits attached)* and the tenant agrees not to amend or modify the lease without the prior written consent of lender *(an estoppel certificate should not impose obligations on the tenant that are not contained in the lease—they are likely to be forgotten).*

5. No rents under the lease have been prepaid, except the current month's rent. The tenant agrees that it shall not prepay any rents under the lease more than one month from the date when such rents are due. *This is okay, if true. Sometimes landlords require payment of the first month's rent when the lease is signed, even though the rent commencement date may not occur until leasehold improvements are finished or a rent fee period has elapsed.* The tenant does not now have or hold any claim or defense against the landlord that might be set off or credited against future accruing rents or might otherwise excuse the tenant's performance under the lease. *Any concessions, tenant improvement allowances, or other credits should be listed.*

6. The tenant has received no notice of a prior sale, transfer, assignment, hypothecation, or pledge of the lease or of the rents secured therein.

There may be an existing mortgage that is being paid off. The tenant should disclose any of which it has received notice.

7. The tenant does not have any outstanding options or rights of first refusal to purchase the premises, or any part thereof, or to purchase or lease any other part of the building, except (state none, if applicable). *This applies to purchase rights, as well as extension or expansion rights. They should be disclosed if they exist.*

8. No actions, whether voluntary or involuntary, are pending against the tenant or any guarantor of the lease under any bankruptcy, insolvency, or similar laws of the United States or any state thereof. *Okay if accurate.*

9. The term of the lease commenced on the _____ day of _____, 20__, and ends on the _____ day of _____, 20__, subject to options to extend, if any, set forth in the lease. *Insert the accurate information.*

10. The current monthly base rental payable by the tenant under the lease is $_____. Percentage rent [is/is not] payable, as provided in the lease. The current estimated monthly payments made by the tenant under the lease in respect of common-area maintenance costs and real estate taxes are $_____ and $_____, respectively. *Insert the accurate information.*

11. The security deposit under the lease is currently $_____. *Insert the accurate information or insert "None" if there is no security deposit.*

12. So long as the loan is outstanding, the tenant shall pay any termination fees payable for the early termination of the lease to the landlord and lender jointly. *An estoppel certificate should not contain new obligations of the tenant—they are likely to be forgotten.*

13. The lender will rely on the representations and agreements made by the tenant herein in connection with the lender's agreement to make the loan, and the tenant agrees that the lender may so rely on such representations and agreements. *This is merely a reminder of the effect of the estoppel certificate.*

Leases sometimes seek to deal with the situation in which the tenant does not promptly sign and return the estoppel certificate. I can attest to the fact that if the landlord is financing or selling a property with many tenants, collecting all of the estoppel certificates on a timely basis can be quite a chore. However, the remedies inserted into the leases can be very onerous. One common remedy is that if the estoppel certificate is not returned within the time specified in the lease, the tenant is deemed to have confirmed all of the statements in the document. Another remedy, which has pretty much the same effect, is that the landlord is authorized to sign the document on the tenant's behalf. With due regard for the landlord's problem, I submit that those remedies should be unacceptable to the tenant.

It should be noted that the estoppel certificates are customarily delivered by the tenant to the landlord, not directly to the lender or to the buyer. There is a good reason for the landlord to want that to happen. A tenant may make a statement that is not true or have a claim the landlord is willing to remedy right away. If the document is delivered to the lender or buyer, it may cause serious problems that a conversation between the landlord and tenant could have avoided. On the other hand, if a landlord who is not very scrupulous receives an estoppel certificate with statements that may hinder its deal, it may be tempted to throw the estoppel certificate in the recycling bin, claim it was never returned, and either sign the original one or take the position with the lender or the buyer that the facts were all admitted.

In representing a lender or buyer who was asked to accept such a document or rely on the lease language that the facts were admitted, I would recommend that it not do so. But who can be certain that the lender or buyer would get or decide to accept that advice? I admit that it is difficult to fashion a remedy for the default in delivering an estoppel certificate, but from a tenant's point of view, the ones described above are not acceptable and the operative language should be deleted from the lease.

SNDAs

SNDA is short for subordination and non-disturbance agreement. If a property leased before a mortgage was in place is later being financed, or if the landlord is refinancing a prior mortgage, then in addition to the estoppel certificate, the lender may well ask for an SNDA. In that connection, let me repeat what I said on pages 41 and 42: If the lease is executed and delivered before the mortgage is, and the mortgagee has notice (by recording of a memorandum of lease) or actual knowledge of the existence of the lease (such as by inspecting the property and seeing the tenant building out the space or conducting its business), the lease has priority; if there is a fore-closure, the lender cannot wipe out the lease. I also discussed the nature of a non-disturbance agreement and what a lender may be willing to agree to and what a tenant requires.

A new lender may not be concerned about the tenant's protection against foreclosure, but the lender has some legitimate concerns that may require the tenant's agreement. For example, it may want the agreements referred to in the estoppel certificate, to which I objected in the italics. It may also want to know that it, rather than the tenant, has the first claims in the event of a casualty loss or a condemnation. Most importantly, however, it will want the tenant to agree to attorn to it in the event of a foreclosure, as discussed on page 43. For those reasons, the lender may want the tenant to subordinate its legal position (as first in time, first in right), but at the same time, the lender will agree to the non-disturbance and recognition, all as discussed above.

Lease forms often provide that the lease will be subordinate to a subse-quent loan, but do not provide for an SNDA from the lender. Some leases state that the tenant will not be disturbed in the event of a foreclosure of a loan by a subsequent lender. Neither of those provisions should satisfy the tenant. The obligation to subordinate should be conditioned on the land-lord obtaining an SNDA from the new lender. The obligation of the tenant to be subordinate is enforceable by the lender, as a third-party beneficiary, but the landlord cannot agree to non-disturbance on behalf of a lender— only the lender can agree to that. The landlord's agreement that the tenant will not be disturbed is meaningless. Whom is the tenant going to sue if the property, which is all that is owned by this landlord, is foreclosed?

Even a small tenant should not be required to give up a priority position without the protection, even if somewhat limited, of the SNDA. And the SNDA should be commercially reasonable in form or, for larger tenants, reasonably acceptable to the tenant.

Lease forms often provide that if the tenant does not sign the SNDA presented by the lender, the landlord is authorized to do so, as attorney-in-fact for the tenant. When representing a tenant, I strongly object to that, not only for the reasons stated above in connection with the estoppel certificate, but also I object to my tenant clients giving a power of attorney to landlords for any purposes. Just as in the case of the estoppel certificate, the tenant and its counsel, and perhaps its broker, should have the right to review and evaluate the agreements that the tenant is being asked to make.

Force Majeure

"Force majeure" is a French phrase that has the following dictionary definition: "an event or effect that cannot be reasonably anticipated or controlled." As examples, we might list strikes, lockouts, labor trouble (whether legal or illegal), civil disorder, failure of power, restrictive governmental laws and regulations, delays in the issuance of building permits or certificates of occupancy by the appropriate governmental authority, riots, insurrections, war, shortages, accidents, casualties, "acts of God," acts caused directly by the other party or its agents, employees, and invitees, or any other cause beyond the reasonable control of a party.

The question is whether the occurrence of any of these events excuses the performance under the lease by the party affected by them. The simple answer is no—unless the lease provides that it does.

Let's take an example unrelated to leasing. A farmer plants his wheat crop in the spring and it starts coming up nicely. Being in need of cash, he enters into a contract to deliver the crop when harvested to the local miller at $5 per bushel. You can figure out what happens next—there is a late summer drought and most of the crop is destroyed. Will the drought excuse the farmer's obligation to deliver the wheat at $5 per bushel? Not on your life! The poor farmer must go on the market and buy wheat, now at $7 per bushel, to deliver it for $5 per bushel, at a loss to him of $2 per bushel (and there were a lot of bushels covered in the contract). The next year, the farmer asks the miller for a provision in the contract that excuses his performance if there is another drought or, perhaps, a flood, or any act of God. "No way!" says the miller. "I need predictability for my business." What does the farmer do? He hedges. He buys a futures contract or an option to buy wheat. He covers his delivery, and he may actually make some money on the board of trade.

Well, there are no futures contracts for lease performance—at least not yet. There is insurance against some of the events, such as fire, windstorm, even flood or earthquake, but not to many of the other events referred to, so the parties need lease language that has the effect of superseding the general legal principle that force majeure does not excuse performance (or excuse prompt performance). Since most leases are written on forms prepared by landlords, it should not be a great surprise that the party whose performance is most often excused (or delay permitted) is the landlord's.

This is not to say that tenants do not also seek force majeure protection and often get it, but with certain exceptions. Those exceptions are (or should be) the tenant's obligation to pay rent and other charges, provide a security deposit when and if required in the lease, provide evidence of insurance required under the lease, surrender the premises when required, or deliver estoppel certificates and SNDAs when required.

Tenant's Financial Statements

Leases usually contain a requirement that the tenant (and its guarantor, if there is one) deliver to the landlord, from time to time, financial statements (preferably audited and certified, but if those are not customarily prepared, statements certified as true and correct by an executive officer of the tenant) so the landlord can, in turn, deliver them to its lender, its prospective lenders, or purchasers. That seemingly innocuous requirement can and often does create disputes and sometimes even kill deals. Of course, there is no problem for publicly held companies; they are quite willing to deliver their annual statements and their other filings with the Security and Exchange Commission. After all, those materials are available to the general public on the Internet.

With privately held companies or with individual proprietorships, the matter is more problematic. These prospective tenants feel that no one should have the right to see their statements. Their reasons might be that they are afraid the information will reach their competitors, or that their income, expenses, assets, liabilities, and net worth are no one's business but their own. They may even have something to hide, but we should not assume that to be the case.

The issue is sometimes resolved with the landlord's agreement to hold the materials in confidence, although it may deliver them to its lender, prospective lenders, or prospective purchasers. There may be a further condition that the documents be delivered to the landlord or, by the landlord to those parties, only if they execute a confidentiality agreement stating that they will not show the materials to anyone, or disclose their contents, except on a need-to-know basis or in the event they are compelled to do so in litigation. I have always wondered about the effectiveness of such agreements. How are they to be enforced? If the tenant knows or suspects that the confidence will be breached, it can sue to enjoin disclosure, but how, in most cases, will it know that? Once the information is disclosed, the cat is out of the bag, as it were. How does a court determine what damages are to be assessed against the revealing party? How does anyone even know who has seen the materials unless the agreement is so tightly written that it does not even pay for the landlord to request the statements?

On occasion, the tenant will agree to deliver the materials, with a confidentiality agreement, directly to the lender or to the prospective lender or purchaser, as the case may be, and not to the landlord at all. The landlord prefers to see the materials before they are delivered to the other party because it can then determine what issues may arise as a result of the contents and develop a strategy for dealing with those issues. Still, the landlord will usually agree to that condition, even though it may have to discuss problems with a lender or buyer without any knowledge of the basis for the discussion.

Some years ago I had a major deal that nearly cratered on this issue. The tenant simply refused to deliver the material to anyone. Here is how we resolved it: The tenant agreed that the lender or buyer could come to its office where that party would be shown the statements. The lender or buyer could ask questions but not copy any documents or take any notes. Neither party was very satisfied with that compromise, but it enabled the deal to go forward. It is a result that might be helpful to you if you have a deal teetering on the edge of a cliff because of this issue.

Landlord's Expenses

Many leases provide, pretty broadly, that the tenant is to reimburse the landlord for certain expenses (including reasonable legal fees). Those expenses might include arbitration or court costs incurred in enforcing the tenant's obligations under the lease; in curing any default by tenant; in connection with appearing, defending, or otherwise participating in any action or proceeding arising from the filing, imposition, contesting, discharging, or satisfaction of any lien or claim for lien; or in defending or otherwise participating in any legal proceedings initiated by or on behalf of the tenant in which the landlord is not adjudicated to be in default under the lease. Those types of expenses are really pretty unlikely to occur.

On the other hand, the lease may provide for the tenant to pay the landlord's expenses incurred in connection with any investigation or review of any conditions or documents in the event the tenant requests the landlord's agreement, approval, or consent to any action of the tenant that may be desired by the tenant or required of the tenant under the lease. The approval or consent provision refers to requests by the tenant for consent to an assignment or sublease, or requests for approval of alterations and of the plans and specifications for alterations, both of which might require the landlord to incur costs for outside lawyers or architects. Those types of expenses are certainly more likely to be incurred by landlords and are thus of concern to tenants.

There are two issues in the landlord expenses section that are frequently the subject of negotiation. The first relates to legal fees for defaults. The tenant wants to have its fees and costs reimbursed if it wins the litigation, either because of its having sued the landlord or because it has been sued. This mutuality is usually agreed to in what is typically referred to as "prevailing party" language. I recently revised my customary lease insert, however, when the following occurred. A landlord client sued a tenant claiming a Default under its lease. Because of some defect in the filing (I did not handle the litigation but I assure you that I am not immune to mistakes), the suit was dismissed, with the landlord being given leave to refile the case. The tenant argued that, because the case was dismissed at its motion, it was entitled to reimbursement of its fee. The client requested a change in the form (that is how leases grow), and I provided that the reimbursement would occur only if there was a decision on the merits of the case (which certainly did not occur there, and would not have occurred even if the landlord had not had the right to refile the action).

The other issue relates to the reimbursement for the cost of obtaining the landlord's consent. Bear in mind that most consents requested under a lease do not involve the landlord in any expense. There are two that do. One is consent relating to construction (actually, that consists of a number of consents—one relating to the right to perform the work, and others relating to the plans or approval of contractors). The other relates to assignment or subletting. Both of these may involve the landlord in costs for professionals outside its organization. If the landlord incurs out-of-pocket expenses for the sole benefit of the tenant, it feels that the tenant should pay for that. The tenant may be willing to pay something, but is concerned about how much it will cost and how the costs may be controlled. A further issue arises if the professionals are inside the landlord's organization, such as in-house counsel. I cannot really recommend a solution here, as the outcomes vary considerably.

Sometimes the tenant asks for reimbursement if its consent is required, or even if it is required to sign an estoppel certificate or an SNDA. Generally, only strong tenants get the landlord to agree to those.

Surrender

What should the condition of the premises be at the end of the term, whether because the lease has expired or because the lease is terminated early by reason of an agreement between the parties or by reason of a default? Most leases state that the tenant must remove its furniture, fixtures, and equipment and repair any damage. Many also make it the landlord's option as to whether the tenant is to remove its alterations or leave them (unless the landlord has agreed otherwise when the alterations were performed). Some leases provide that if the tenant removes alterations, it must restore the premises to their condition prior to the making of the alterations. After all, the landlord will argue, if the tenant tore out some building fixtures or walls to install its alteration, should it not be required to put the original fixtures or walls back in so that the premises do not need a lot of work by the landlord in order to relet them? On the other hand, the tenant will argue that restoration may be very expensive and the next tenant may not have a need for those fixtures or walls anyway, or that the landlord may intend to rip out all the leasehold improvements and alterations anyway. This is a matter that should be resolved by the parties, and perhaps the decision should actually be made when the tenant proposes making an alteration that includes removal of existing fixtures or walls. Of course, the landlord will probably not know at the time the alteration is installed what might be required by a subsequent tenant, but it probably can make a pretty educated guess based on the nature of the proposed alteration.

Then there is the exception for "reasonable wear and tear" or "ordinary wear and tear"—both of which are acceptable, but I prefer "reasonable." Premises get older and wear out even if the tenant performs all the required maintenance, repairs, and replacements. Of course, wear and tear should not be used to enable the tenant to escape the consequences of its default in not maintaining the premises as required under the lease, so some language to that effect may be appropriate. In addition, damage resulting from a tenant's particular use of the premises, such as damage resulting from a particular manufacturing process (even if permitted under the lease), should not, from the landlord's point of view, be deemed "reasonable wear and tear."

What about loss by fire or other casualty? If the landlord is obligated under the lease to restore after a casualty loss, then "or loss by fire or other casualty" should be added after "reasonable wear and tear." On the other hand, if the tenant is required to restore, it should not be excused from doing so by reason of the fact that the lease has ended (possibly because the loss occurred toward the end of the term), but the parties might agree, at that time, that the insurance proceeds (plus any shortfall) will be paid over to the landlord in lieu of the tenant's restoration of the premises.

Notices

You may wonder why I consider notices to be so important as to cover the topic in this book. It is because if notices are not received in a timely manner, the party receiving the notice will not have the opportunity to correct the problem of which it is being notified. On the other hand, if one of the parties has a right that it must exercise by giving notice on or before a specific date, if the notice arrives late, the right may be gone.

Notice sections generally provide for various ways to give notice, such as personal delivery, registered or certified mail, commercial courier, or by fax or e-mail with a follow-up notice by mail. I have pretty strong views about mailed notices. If I send them by registered or certified mail, a receipt is required, and if it is to be signed by the addressee only, the postal service might have to make several attempts to deliver. Even if the item can be signed for by any responsible person, I have found that it takes the postal service a long time to get the item to the address and a long time to get the receipt back so the sender knows when the addressee accepted the notice and whether it is effective for its purposes. If receipt or refusal is the trigger (and I believe it should be, except as discussed on page 119), the sender does not know for some time whether the trigger has been pulled and it can act on the fact that the notice is given or deemed given. This will delay the sender's right to file suit, which may have substantial consequences, especially if the recipient has filed for bankruptcy relief before the notice is received. In that situation, not only is the sender subject to the automatic stay (see page 99) but, if the lease has not been effectively terminated due to a default before the filing of the bankruptcy, the lease may be an asset of the bankrupt estate, with considerable bad consequences for the landlord.

A better course, in my view, would be personal delivery (although I am somewhat skeptical about who might actually be doing the delivering and who may actually be the recipient), or commercial courier, with receipt. Except in extraordinary circumstances, the notice will be there the next business day and the sender will be able to confirm delivery with very little difficulty.

The exception is the exercise of an option or right, of which notice must be given on or before a specified date. In that case, sending the notice by, say, FedEx, which may fly the document to Memphis even if the notice is being sent across town, may not get it there by the next business day if there is a major snow storm or other force majeure event that keeps its planes out of the sky. I believe that such notices should be effective as of the date they are sent.

What about fax notices? It seems to me that fax is rapidly going out of fashion and may soon be as obsolete as the pony express. Besides, there is no assurance that a notice sent to a common fax machine actually reached the right person. I am not very comfortable with e-mail notices either. Hit a wrong key and the notice is never received by the intended addressee, and the sender will not know it since it may have gone to another person who simply deleted it instead of responding. Another problem is that it may have been missed in the storm of e-mails each of us receives every day or it may have been blocked by a spam or junk mail filter.

Rent

There are only two things I can think of that are universal to all leases: the provision for the use and occupancy of the premises by the tenant and the payment of rent to the landlord.

The word "rent" covers a lot of payments by the tenant to the landlord, and most leases specify in some way that all rent, additional rent, and other charges are referred to as rent. That is because many states provide for expedited proceedings to evict defaulting tenants and allow the court in those proceedings to include a judgment for rent. If certain charges are not characterized as rent, the landlord would have to bring a separate, non-expedited action to collect them.

The specified periodic rent, often referred to as "base rent" or "minimum rent," is set forth in all leases. I will refer to it here as "base rent." Unlike other forms of rent that will be discussed in this section, the lease provisions dealing with the base rent do not differ based on the type of lease. Annual base rent (and the monthly installments) or monthly base rent is customarily set forth in the lease. If specific periodic increases in base rent have been agreed to as the financial escalation during the initial term or any extensions or expansions (such as percentage increases), those increases are described or the actual amounts set out in a schedule. Other forms of financial escalation are more complicated, as we shall see.

Cost-of-Living Adjustments

Sometimes leases of various types provide for increasing base rent based on increases of the cost of living. The most common way to do so is to use a consumer price index published by the Bureau of Labor Statistics of the U.S. Department of Labor. It is important to note that the bureau prepares a number of different indices. For example, there are indices for "All Urban Consumers—CPI-U" and for "Urban Wage Earners and Clerical Workers—CPI-W." Each of those indices is published on a national basis and on regional bases. The lease should specify which index should be used. Then again, the indices have been published over the years with different base years. The base at this writing is 1982–1984=100.

A lease using CPI-U or CPI-W should specify the comparison years or months to be used for calculating the increase in the rent (landlord-drafted leases usually provide that rent is not to be reduced). As the base for that purpose, I usually specify the month that is two months before the beginning of the measuring period and two months before the effective date of the increase. I do that because that will be the rate available when the rent bumps up. For example, if the rent is to start on June 1, 2014 and the increase in rent is to occur one year later, I would provide that the CPI for April 2014 should be compared with the CPI for April 2015 to determine the percentage of increase, and so on year by year.

Another possible index is the gross domestic product (GDP) deflator, published by the Bureau of Economic Analysis of the U.S. Department of Commerce. That index compares the levels of GDP between two specified years or months. The brokers or the drafter of the lease may examine the various indices to determine which one has historically been more favorable to its client, but usually that does not happen, especially on the average lease deal. Generally one of the CPI-U indices is referred to.

Also, the parties might agree to use a cost-of-living adjustment, but to predicate the rent increase on a stated percentage of the increase in the index, such as 50 percent of the increase during the period. That is a way to compromise the financial escalation.

In the years since the end of the high inflation experienced in the 1980s, cost-of-living adjustments have fallen out of favor and specified increases have become more common. However, one cannot be certain that inflation will be low forever, so we might expect that one day cost-of-living adjustments will reemerge in leases. On the other hand, in the year 2010, there was considerable fear of deflation, which has not been experienced in the United States since the Great Depression. Might not some tenants seek a cost-of-living adjustment to reduce the rent if the applicable index declines?

Market Rent

Sometimes the parties are unable to agree as to what the rent amount should be at some future date. This frequently happens in the case of a ground lease, which generally has a very long term. The situation may also arise when there is an option to extend or an option to lease additional or other premises. The parties may specify that market rent will apply. Unless the landlord and the tenant are very specific as to what market rent means and how it is to be determined, they may find that instead of specifying a reasonable means of determining the rent, they have created a monster. If the lease only provides that the parties are to agree on the market rent, even if they must act in good faith, they will probably have created what is known in law as "an illusory agreement," which is not enforceable because it is simply an agreement to agree. They can litigate with one another, but the fact remains that no judge is going to want to decide what the rent should be in the given situation.

In order to determine market rent, the parties must first define the "relevant market." This is not as easy as it sounds. Take a retail situation, for example. Assume the tenant is seeking to lease a store on Fifth Avenue and 53rd Street in New York City. How comparable is rent for similar space on 53rd and Lexington Avenue or even Fifth Avenue and 43rd Street? How comparable is the rent for a 1,000 square foot space on Fifth Avenue and 53rd Street with a 10,000 square foot space in the same area. Even if the reader is not familiar with New York geography, I think nearly everyone knows that midtown Fifth Avenue is an upscale retail area. Lexington Avenue south of midtown is not.

Likewise, in an office lease situation, if the space is in a 40-year-old building, how do the rents compare with a new one across the street, let alone in another area of the city? Perhaps the only comparable space is space in the same building, but even there, some tenants have long-term leases and their rents may have been negotiated a long time ago, whereas some are new tenants. Besides, the landlord may be quoting an even higher rent for tenants looking for space when the market rent is to be determined. The situation may be easier in the industrial/warehouse situation, but not necessarily so.

When and if the relevant market is agreed to, there is still the question of what constitutes the rent. That is not an easy answer either. If the tenant is paying rent on a net basis, the question to be answered is fairly straightforward. What is the net rent for the relevant market at the time the market rent is being determined? However, what is the market rent if the tenant is paying a gross base rent and a percentage of certain costs over a base? Remember that in this situation, the base costs are included in the gross base rent at the time the lease is first negotiated. Assume that the gross rent is $25, but the taxes, insurance, and operating expenses (pass-throughs) included in that gross rent is $10, and that the base is $10. If in 10 years, the market gross rent is $35 because the pass-throughs have increased to $15 (the other $5 is simply a market increase), unless the base for the pass-throughs is increased to $15, the tenant is not really getting a market rate; it is overpaying by $5.

There is yet another variable to be considered: what if other tenants have had concessions? Perhaps they have had some free rent or have had new build-out, which is not contemplated in connection with the current deal as to which the new rent is being determined. Landlords are not giving those concessions away for nothing. It is factored into the rent the other tenant will be paying over the balance of its term. In other words, the "comparable rent" is a rent that includes the amortization (with some profit factor) of the concessions. Unless your tenant is to get concessions of similar value, its "market rent" should be reduced by the amount the concessions are being factored into the supposedly comparable rent.

Finally, it is very likely that the landlord would have to pay a commission on a new lease, so the market rate includes a factor for that commission. Unless the tenant rep broker was able to get the landlord to agree to pay a commission on extension (which is pretty unusual), the landlord is getting a great deal if it gets a rent that has a commission factored in but does not have to pay one. That is why you sometimes see that the actual rent is to be 95 percent of market rent.

All right, let us assume that the parties have agreed to the appropriate market and considered all the factors affecting the rate of rent described above, and they have further agreed that they will attempt in good faith to decide on the applicable rent considering all those matters. What should the lease provide in the event the landlord and tenant are unable to agree on the market rent?

Obviously some third party or parties will have to make the decision. The parties might agree on arbitration. That is a pretty thorough way to have the decision made. Each party does an investigation of rents in the market, considering all the factors. Then there is an evidentiary hearing before one or more arbitrators (who are paid by the parties), and the decision made by the arbitrator or arbitrators is binding on the parties. The parties will have been represented by lawyers and will have had expert witnesses testify. It would have to be quite a deal to justify all those expenses.

Another approach is to have experts make the decision. Each party hires its own expert and each expert renders his or her opinion as to the market rent. Obviously, it is very unlikely that they will come up with the same number, so some method of resolving the difference will still have to be considered. One alternative is what is called "baseball arbitration." The experts (or even the parties themselves) come up with an amount, and a third party (also an expert) decides which is closest to the proper number, and that is the market rent. In an alternative to "baseball arbitration," the lease may provide that if the higher amount is within 10 percent of the lower amount, the two are averaged for the answer. If not, a third expert, selected by the first two, decides.

There is still another issue to be resolved. Who are to be the experts? I have often seen leases that designate appraisers as experts. Well, those people may know how to find comparables to determine value for sale or financing purposes, but they are extremely unlikely to know what the rents are in a given market since that information is not publicly available. Really, only brokers can be expected to know that because they are dealing with those numbers every day. So the parties might designate brokers with a certain level of experience who are unrelated to either party and have not done business with them; that is the method I prefer.

When all is said and done, when the parties see how long these procedures take and how much the experts will cost, and understand that even at its best, the decision-making process will be flawed, they usually end up agreeing on the market rent themselves.

Some parties may object to a binding determination of market rent. Their thinking is that they do not want to be bound unless they feel that the outcome is fair. Of course, that undermines the entire system created to determine the applicable rent and if either party has the right to reject the determination, that makes the entire provision, however carefully drafted, illusory.

Multi-owner Expenses

If the property containing the premises is part of a larger complex with multiple owners, such as an industrial park, an office park, or a retail center, there is likely to be a declaration of easements, covenants, and restrictions that was recorded by the developer of the park or center and that requires the property owners to pay their share of certain costs, such as the cost of maintenance of landscaping, private roads, common parking areas, storm-water retention or detention facilities, private utilities, and the like. Those costs, whether billed directly to the tenant or paid by the landlord and re-billed to the tenant, will be the tenant's expense, as pass-throughs (see page 132 for a further discussion of pass-throughs).

PART III

LEASE PROVISIONS SPECIFIC TO CERTAIN TYPES OF LEASES

Earlier in this book, I touched on some of the issues to be discussed below. Although I have given a foretaste of those issues, I feel that it is appropriate to discuss them in greater detail. For example, although I just discussed matters relating to rent, I am dealing with it again because certain items that make up rent, other than those discussed above, tend to be specific to certain types of leases. Thus percentage rent is specific to retail leasing, as are the payment of certain common-area expenses. Industrial/warehouse and office leases may also provide for the payment of common-area expenses, but office leases customarily provide for the payment of operating expenses instead. These are all pass-throughs and are deemed to be rent for the reasons expressed on page 120. Anyway, a little review is not a bad thing.

Percentage Rent

I discussed percentage rent briefly on page 27. To reiterate, percentage rent is rent calculated based on the sales from retail premises. Of course, not all retail leases provide for percentage rent; many have other means of protecting the landlord from inflation. Some have specified amounts or percentage increase in the stated rent, either annually or at other times, or upon the exercise of an option to extend or expand, and some provide for those financial escalations and also for percentage rent. For example, a lease might provide for a fixed minimum rent of $60,000 per year for the first year, $61,800 for the second year (being a 3 percent increase), and so on, and still require the tenant to pay percentage rent. That usually occurs when the percentage rent breakpoint is so high that the landlord does not really expect to collect percentage rent unless the tenant does exceptionally well or inflation is very high.

So how does percentage rent work? Let's assume a lease to a clothing store in which the percentage rent is the only financial escalation, that the annual stated rent is $50,000, and that the agreed percentage is 5 percent. Is the tenant paying 5 percent of all sales, or just sales above an agreed "break point"? In our lease, the "natural" break point is $1 million. How is that determined? In the absence of a stated rent, when the tenant has sold $1 million of goods and services, it will be obligated to pay $50,000 in percentage rent. However, the stated rent is a minimum rent, which is to be paid whether the tenant sells $1,000 or $1 million, so the parties agree that if the tenant sells more than $1 million, it must pay additional rent of the excess based on the 5 percent agreed to.

Of course, the percentage to be paid by tenants will vary from deal to deal, and some types of retailers pay more and some pay less. Drug stores and supermarkets tend to pay less percentage rent, if any, while tenants who sell at substantial markups tend to pay more.

Nor is it unusual for a lease to provide that the tenant is to pay a stated percentage on all its sales and provide for a deduction for the stated rent. Also, the percentage may vary depending on the volume of sales, sometimes increasing and sometimes decreasing. Thus a lease might provide as follows: "The tenant shall pay, as percentage rent, 5 percent of gross sales until gross sales exceed $1 million, and 6 percent of gross sales in excess of $1 million until gross sales exceed $2 million, and 7 percent of gross sales in excess of $2 million. The tenant shall be entitled to a credit against percentage rent in an amount equal to the fixed minimum rent paid by the tenant." Note that, as drafted, if the fixed minimum rent is abated during a part of a year (such as by reason of a fire), but the tenant's sales are excellent during the balance of the year, the landlord still gets the full rent (it could accomplish the same thing by adjusting the break point, but that is not as sneaky).

When is percentage rent paid? The tenant prefers that it be paid at the end of the year, preferably the calendar year after the Christmas season. The landlord will want it paid in monthly installments, with an adjustment at the end of each lease year, for three reasons. First, it wants the use of the money. Second, it may be concerned about the credit of the tenant. And third, if the lease starts in the middle of the year, it will receive a bump in the payment right after the Christmas season and the downward adjustment may not occur until the following June, giving the landlord the use of more of the tenant's money.

Percentage rent is usually paid based on the tenant's gross sales as defined in the lease. Typically, gross sales means the gross amount charged for all sales made or services rendered on or from the premises, including sales made by licensees or concessionaires. Each sale is valued at the actual sales price charged the customer and reported in full in the month the sale occurs, even if the sale is a credit or installment sale, if full payment is not received at the time of the sale, or if the goods are not delivered until a later date. Usually the tenant negotiates for exclusions from gross sales, some of which are not controversial—but others generate a lot of discussion. Some of the noncontroversial exclusions may even be included in the landlord's lease form. The landlord usually agrees to exclude sales taxes, returned goods, goods transferred to the tenant's other stores where the transfer is not for the purpose of consummating a sale, and sales out of the ordinary course of business, such as sales in bulk. Sometimes the landlord will agree to exclude sales to employees at cost or at a substantial discount. Landlords will balk at excluding charges made by credit card companies, as that is simply a cost of doing business, but if a merchant extends credit itself, exclusion for bad debts may be agreed to, subject to a maximum percentage of sales. If a tenant has more than one store and the sale occurs in the other store and the goods are delivered from the premises, percentage rent should not be payable in both places, but the parties will have to decide which landlord gets the credit for the sale. If goods are purchased at another store but returned at this one, which store gets to deduct the sale? If goods are sold on the Internet but delivered from the premises, percentage rent is often charged, and it might also be charged if the item is ordered online at the premises but delivered directly to the customer's home. There is also an issue regarding gift certificates. Are they included when and where they are sold or when and where they are redeemed? What if they are sold at another store and redeemed at this one, or vice versa?

As can be seen, just finalizing the definition of gross sales can be very difficult and time-consuming, but then we move on to the issue of record keeping. What good is agreeing to the definition of gross sales if there is no foolproof way to assure that all sales are properly recorded? The lease form might specify some method of recording sales, but in the negotiations the tenant announces that it customarily uses another method and changing its methods can be extremely expensive; further, the tenant does not want to have different methods for different stores. So how does the tenant's method ensure that the proper amount of percentage rent will be paid? Certainly the tenant has a strong interest in knowing how the store is doing, but that does not mean that it is averse to hiding the facts from the landlord (and perhaps the sales tax authorities). And once the parties agree on the method of record keeping, the lease will also provide the landlord the right to audit the tenant's records to make certain that it is not being cheated, with penalties built in for underpayment.

Providing for percentage rent builds an entirely new administrative hassle into rent payment, so it is no wonder that many landlords try to avoid percentage rent and to rely on other methods of financial escalation to protect their profits, but that does not mean that percentage rent will go away.

Pass-Throughs

Pass-throughs consist of all the expenses customarily incurred by the landlord for which the tenant is liable under the lease, either by paying the expense directly or by reimbursing the landlord for expenses paid by the landlord. Pass-throughs differ from one type of lease to another, and also differ depending on the leasing situation in each type of lease.

Ground Leases
In situations where the tenant leases a piece of ground from the landlord and builds its own building, the tenant generally owns title to the building, at least for the term of the lease. Whether it owns the building or not, the tenant typically pays all the costs of maintaining and insuring it, and to restore the building after a casualty loss. The lease will also require the tenant to pay all the real estate taxes pertaining to the land and building.

Industrial/Warehouse Leases

Single Tenant

Similarly, if the tenant leases an industrial/warehouse building or a big-box retail store, or any freestanding building in which it is the only tenant, the lease—particularly if it is a long-term lease—may provide that the tenant undertake all of the same responsibilities. These are true triple-net leases, with the tenant paying for the taxes, property and liability insurance, and maintenance, repairs, and replacements. These leases were sometimes called "net and bond" leases because of their similarity to coupon bonds since the landlord does nothing other than to collect the rent, pay the debt service if there is a mortgage, and keep the balance of the proceeds. This is the least complex situation for the landlord, but let us add some complexity.

Assume that the building is somewhat old and may during the course of the lease need a new roof, or that the rooftop HVAC unit is old and may need replacement during the term. The parking lot may need resurfacing. The tenant is willing to pay for repairs and maintenance but not for replacements. Further, it is not willing to pay for structural problems that may result from the age of the building. Here is where you get into some negotiation. Perhaps the landlord is willing to pay to replace the roof, replace the HVAC equipment, or resurface the parking lot, provided the tenant has diligently inspected and repaired it as long as it can be made useful, but if the lease term is long enough or the tenant has options to extend, or even if it extends the lease by amendment, the landlord will want the tenant to be obligated to pay for subsequent replacements, on the theory that the tenant has used up the useful life of the replaced item. An alternative is to provide that the tenant will pay for the replacement over time, based on the useful life of the replaced item, plus some interest factor to reimburse the landlord for having advanced the cost of the replacement. Of course, the tenant will not want to pay any of it.

As to structure problems, landlords tend to refuse to take on the responsibility on the theory that the building is old and the tenant is paying a rental based on an old building. Problems that arise are most likely not caused by defects in the original construction. The risk is minimal (although I have represented clients in situations where structural walls started bowing out), so if the tenant is afforded the opportunity to do an inspection, it is likely to accept the landlord's position.

Some net leases provide that the tenant is to carry the property insurance and be obligated to rebuild the premises after a loss. There are issues here, too. If the tenant carries the property insurance, it should also be required to carry the business income insurance to provide proceeds for the payment of the rent, since it is cheaper to carry business income insurance along with the property insurance than to carry it separately. If that is the case, the lease should not provide for rent abatement since the tenant and not the landlord will have the insurance proceeds applicable to the rents (and the business income insurance should cover all rent, including taxes, and not just the base rent). An interesting side issue is that most leases drafted in this manner do not deal with the situation in which there is an uninsured casualty, such as earthquake or flood.[1] The tenant's obligation to rebuild under those circumstances may come as quite a surprise to it.

There might also be rail service that serves more than one property with a single rail spur. Any maintenance costs imposed by the railroad will have to be properly allocated among the rail users only so that if there are three buildings in the complex that could use the rail service, but only two use it, those costs will have to be allocated to them, either by usage or by square footage of the served building.

Multiple Tenants

Moving up in complexity, we have the multi-tenant industrial/warehouse leases—anything from a two-tenant building, each with direct access to the parking areas and its own truck docks, to those with numerous tenants, sometimes with common corridors and common truck docks. Certainly the landlord will have to be more involved in the operation of this type of project. The landlord and not the tenants will be paying the taxes, carrying the property insurance (and also liability and other insurance), and performing maintenance, repairs, and replacements (except for interior ones and for

---

1. Although earthquake and flood insurance are available in earthquake or flood hazard areas, they are not available in areas of minimal risk, even though such losses are possible there as well. Further, earthquake insurance, where available, is very expensive and the coverage may not be sufficient to repair a major loss.

damage caused by the tenant). Further, the landlord and not the tenant will be contesting tax assessments, and that will involve costs that the landlord will seek to pass on to the tenant. In addition, the landlord has to perform the management function or hire an outside manager. The landlord will look to the tenants to pay their respective share of all those costs, either on a net lease basis or as part of their gross rent, but with stops. Thus, these leases typically require tenants to pay their pro rata share (sometimes referred to as proportionate share) of taxes, the landlord's insurance, the maintenance expenses, and assessments imposed by the association that maintains the common areas of the business park containing the building within which the premises are located.

Stops are discussed in some detail above (see page 22), but to reiterate, stops are the amount in a gross lease over which the tenant pays its share of the applicable expense. Theoretically, the base rent includes a factor for taxes and common-area (or operating) expenses, which include insurance and maintenance, payable for the year in which the base rent is determined (which may be the first year of the term, the immediately prior year, or even the year following, if the pass-throughs do not begin until the year after that), so the hedge against inflation consists of the tenant's paying for those expenses to the extent that they exceed the amount for that base year. Sometimes the base amount is a specified amount, such as $3 per square foot for taxes and $.50 per square foot for common-area (or operating) expenses, or the amount might be specified as the square footage amounts multiplied by the square footage—each is a specified or calculable number. That is fine if the specified amounts represent the actual or realistically anticipated costs, but if the specified amounts are less than the actual or anticipated costs, the tenant will be overpaying *every year during the entire term* by the amount of the difference. Thus it is imperative that the tenant's broker determine what the actual or anticipated costs will be.

Some leases state that the tenant will pay its pro rata share of the excess over a particular year, such as "taxes in excess of the taxes assessed against the property [or payable] for the year 2013" and "maintenance costs in excess of those paid or incurred by the landlord in the year 2013." There are things to be considered in that situation too. What if the taxes for 2013 were not fully assessed because the building on the property is new or because the owner got relief due to economic hardship? In that situation, the tenant will be overcharged for taxes fully assessed in each of the subsequent years during the entire term. Likewise, if maintenance costs were reduced because the building or the equipment was under a warranty that provided for free repairs for a year or the expenses were not for a fully occupied building, and that reduction was reflected in the base, the tenant would again be overcharged in subsequent years.

Some of the same issues apply in multi-tenant situations as applied in the single-tenant situation. What if the landlord incurs expenses for roof replacement or other "capital expenses"? Are the tenants to be billed some share of those costs? If so, should the costs be amortized, and over what period and with what interest factor? Here is a zinger: what if there are several buildings in the complex with common parking areas but obviously separate roofs? Should the tenants in Building B be required to pay for the replacement, or even just the repair, of the roof of Building A, especially if Building A is 10 years older than Building B?

That brings us to another complicated issue—the definition of "pro rata share." Pro rata share is usually defined as a percentage calculated by dividing the rentable area of the premises by the total rentable area of the building (or the property), and that works in most situations. However, take the situation where there are two equally sized spaces, one of which is a warehouse with one small dinky office (Tenant 1) and the other (Tenant 2) is 25 percent warehouse and 75 percent fancy executive offices. Let's assume that the tax assessor in that jurisdiction is efficient and will discover the difference by inspecting the property or even just looking at the building permits—it is not a secret. Is it fair to charge Tenant 1 50 percent of the total tax? A better question is, is it appropriate to charge Tenant 2 only 50 percent of the tax? The answer to both questions is no. Here is what frequently happens: the landlord charges 50 percent of the tax to Tenant 1 and charges 75 percent of the tax to Tenant 2. This is known as "double dipping." Is it fair? Is it right? Of course not. Does it occur? Certainly. The broker representing Tenant 1 has a duty to try to protect its client from the old double dip, but it is not easy—he or she must first be aware of the risk. It is even more difficult to protect Tenant 1 if it leases the property before

Tenant 2 comes into the picture, and perhaps when the Tenant 2 space is still leased to a company with its own dinky office.

As I noted above (see page 136), in a multibuilding complex, there might be separate pro rata shares for separate expenses, so taxes, insurance, and parking lot maintenance may be one pro rata share, but roof replacement and other building maintenance expenses may be shared on a different basis.

One more word about pro rata shares: some leases will define pro rata share in terms of "leased and occupied area" rather than "rentable area." This is terribly unfair to tenants because it requires the existing tenants to pay the expenses for unleased space. There is an issue here for landlords. How is the landlord going to recoup expenses paid only for leased spaces? That can be handled by grossing up, as will be discussed under "Office Leases"(see page 142).

Taxes

Let's move on to taxes. The issues with taxes relate to all kinds of leases, not just industrial/warehouse leases, but this is as good a place as any to discuss them.

Taxes applicable to the property are a major expense and can increase substantially during the term of a lease. Landlords are very eager to pass that expense on to tenants, either as part of their base rent or as a pass-through, but what taxes should or should not be passed through? Certainly real estate taxes are a valid pass-through, but which year's real estate taxes? In states where taxes are paid in the year in which they are assessed, that is a fairly easy question to answer. However, in Illinois and in several other states, taxes are assessed on one year and payable the next. In fact, the amount of the 2013 taxes will not even be determined until sometime in 2014, which creates special problems in those states. Do the tenants pay based on the taxes that are assessed in a specific year or based on those that are payable in that year? If payable, the landlord collects less of the taxes it has to pay for the term of the lease; if assessed, the landlord has to figure out how to collect for taxes payable during the year after the lease term has ended. I will not belabor this because it is a problem unique to those states with that crazy system.

Another tax is the special assessment, usually for an improvement performed by the municipality or county, such as a road or alley improvement.
Those assessments are usually payable up front or in installments with interest. Landlords look to collect those assessments from the tenants, but the
tenants want to pay only those installments that would fall due during the
term of their leases, whether the landlord pays up front or not. There may
also be special taxes for transportation or sewage or drainage districts, which
are customarily included in the definition of taxes. Some jurisdictions have
rent taxes, and those are customarily passed on to the tenants. If there are
great variations in the amount of rent payable by different tenants, those
paying lower rents will want the landlord to bill it for the taxes on its rent,
but those paying higher rents will want the landlord to aggregate the rent
taxes and charge all the tenants on a pro rata basis.

Landlords frequently use the tax definition section to provide for the
tenant's payment of the cost of contesting the tax assessment, and tenants
usually seek to limit the amount of their charge to the savings they realize.
Tenants will also want to receive their pro rata share of any refund. But
how will they ever know there was a refund, especially if it is paid after
the lease expires?

There are usually certain exclusions from the definition of taxes. Those
are federal income taxes, state or local net income taxes, federal excess
profits taxes, and franchise, capital stock, and federal or state estate or
inheritance taxes of the landlord. Note that gross income taxes are not
excluded. There is, however, an exception to the exclusion, which is for
taxes that are subsequently imposed on the landlord and are measured by
or based in whole or in part on the lease, the premises, the property, or
the rent, to the extent that those taxes would be payable if the property
were the only property of the landlord. In many states, property taxes have
reached what is considered unacceptable levels, and some day those states
may undertake to pay a larger share of local costs out of statewide revenue,
particularly for schools. Based on that, new state taxes may be passed with
the condition that property taxes be reduced. The purpose of the exception
to the exclusions is to make the landlord whole if it pays less property tax
but has to pay a substituted or increased income or other state tax. How

this will play out if the taxation method is changed as described cannot be predicted with certainty.

Some landlords seek to include a provision in the tax section providing for the grossing up of taxes if the taxes are reduced due to substantial vacancy on the property. "Grossing up" will be defined and described on page 142.

Tenants sometimes ask for maximums or caps on pass-throughs or on their annual increases. That is understandable, since tenants like to quantify their expenses. The problems for landlords are that some expenses, such as taxes, insurance, and snow removal, are totally out of the landlord's control, and that it is difficult to estimate even the initial cost of items that are nominally within the landlord's control but may increase over the term because of inflation or other factors. When one considers that pass-throughs exist to protect landlords from the effects of inflation and that they are supposed to reflect actual costs (and not profit to landlords), caps do not make much sense. However, we can still expect them to be requested and sometimes agreed to by landlords.

Office Leases

If you think that multi-tenant industrial/warehouse lease pass-throughs are complex, follow me as I move on to office leases, which typically provide for the payment, on a net basis, or as a payment of costs in excess of a stop, of "taxes" and "operating expenses." As to taxes, the issues are similar to those in multi-tenant industrial/warehouse leases, which are discussed above. As to operating expenses, however, we are in an entirely new ball game, a most expansive list of items for which the landlord charges the tenants. I will digress from my usual practice of not including lease language by quoting, at length, the definition of operating expenses in an actual lease form. Then I will discuss the problems that I would raise if I were representing a tenant and encountered this language:

"Operating Expenses" means all expenses, paid or incurred on behalf of the Landlord in respect of the ownership, management, operation and maintenance of the Property which, in accordance with generally accepted accounting principles as applied to the operation of first class office building properties, are properly chargeable to the ownership, management, operation and maintenance of the Property including, without limitation, employees (including the amount of any social security taxes, unemployment insurance contributions and "fringe benefits"), insurance premiums, fuel costs and utility costs, property owners association assessments, management fees and repairs to the Property, replacements of Property and Building components (except footings, floor slabs, exterior walls, columns and structural portions of the roof) amortized on a straight line basis over the useful life of the replaced component (which useful life shall be reasonably determined by the contractor replacing the same). Operating Expenses shall also specifically include the costs, as reasonably amortized by Landlord with interest at the rate of 18% per annum on the unamortized amount, of any capital improvement which reduces other Operating Expenses, but only in an amount not to exceed in any one year the reduction of such expense for that year. Operating Expenses shall not include: (1) any interest expense on mortgages placed upon the Property; (2) franchise or income taxes imposed upon Landlord; (3) the cost of any work or service performed in any instance for any tenant (including the Tenant) at the cost of such tenant; (4) expenses incurred by Landlord as a result of a fire or other casualty or as a result of a taking by way of eminent domain; (5) expenses incurred in leasing or procuring new tenants; (6) legal expenses in enforcing the terms of any leases; or (7) wages, salaries or other compensation paid to any executive employee above the grade of building superintendent. If the Building is not fully occupied during any Year, the variable Operating Expenses for that year shall be equitably adjusted as though the Building were fully occupied. Further, if Landlord is not furnishing any particular work or service (the cost of which if performed by Landlord would constitute an Operating Expense) to a tenant who had undertaken to perform such work or service in lieu of its performance by Landlord, Operating Expenses shall be deemed for the purposes of this Section to be increased by an amount equal to the additional Operating Expenses which would reasonably been incurred by Landlord if it had at its own expense furnished such work or service to such tenant."

Sorry about that (although you brokers should get used to reading stuff like that), but now let's pick it apart.

Note that there is language as to what is included generally, then there are examples of the things that are included, next there are exclusions, and finally there are some provisions for what is referred to as "grossing up."

The general inclusion language has two problems. First, it includes "ownership" expenses. Those are not listed in the examples, but some are, in fact, listed among the exclusions, as items 1, 2, 5, 6, and 7. Why, however, should *any* ownership expenses be paid by the tenants? Should the tenants have to pay for the ownership entity's accountant in preparing its financial statements or tax returns? More importantly, should it have to pay interest on non-mortgage loans or principal on any loans at all? Ownership expenses should not be passed on to tenants—period! The second problem with the general inclusion language is that it states that generally accepted accounting principles (GAAP) should be used to determine what is properly applied to the ownership, management, operation, and maintenance of the property. I am not an accountant and thus not very familiar with GAAP, but it seems to me that a better standard than GAAP would be "reasonable management practices," or words to that effect.

Now we have a series of examples. Note that they are examples only. Other items that may fall within the general inclusion language are not excluded unless they are listed in the exclusion section. The example that pops out is the reference to management. This is a blank check for the landlord. There is no limit on what the landlord may charge for management, whether it does the management itself or contracts with an outside manager (the boss's proverbial brother-in-law?). The management fee should be capped, either here or in additional exclusions, which I will discuss on page 142. The next items relate to capital expenditures—not defined here, but often limited to what must be depreciated rather than expensed under applicable tax laws. This language requires the tenant to pay capital expenditures, amortized over their useful life, as determined by the contractor doing the work (some leases provide for a much faster amortization). Tenants might object to paying for any capital items at all, and this is an area for negotiation. The language specifically provides for amortization of cost-cutting capital expenditures (albeit at an unreasonably high rate of interest), but only to the extent of the savings. Here the language is more generous to tenants than you may see in other leases, which do not have such a limitation.

Let us skip the exclusions for the moment, as they will be discussed below. Suffice it to say that they are inadequate. We will move on to grossing up. Strangely, this language is not unfair to tenants, although many tenants (and their brokers) do not wholly understand the concept and think it is a blank check for landlords to double dip. I often use the following example in explaining this language:

An office building has 20,000 square feet of rentable area. Half of the building is leased to an office tenant and the other half is vacant. The pro rata share of the tenant with the leased space is 50 percent. Only the leased space is cleaned by the landlord's janitor service, which costs $1 per square foot per year. The janitor service is, to the landlord, an expense that varies with the level of occupancy of the property. Without the grossing up language in the lease, the tenant occupying 10,000 square feet would pay 50 percent of the $10,000 cost for the service, or $5,000, even though the cost of cleaning its own space is actually $10,000. It is a windfall for the tenant and the landlord has to pay the balance even though it gets no benefit from the cleaning. The same principle applies even if the other space is leased, but to a business such as a bank, which does its own cleaning because of its security concerns.

Now let us move on to exclusions. I have my own list of exclusions, which I will share with you. Some of them cover the same ground as items 1–7 in the language above, but here they are:

1. costs to the Landlord of any work or services performed in any instances for any tenant (including the Tenant) at the cost of such tenant;

2. capital expenses (except for costs of any capital improvements made or installed for the purpose of reducing operating expenses—and then only to the extent of such reduction in expenses—or made or installed pursuant to governmental law enacted after the date hereof, which shall be amortized in accordance with generally accepted accounting principles consistently applied);

3. wages, salaries, and other benefits for staff above the level of building manager;

4. any expenses or costs associated with bringing the property into compliance with any law, ordinance, or code in effect as of the date of this lease;

5. costs of any service furnished to any other occupant of the property that the landlord does not provide to the tenant hereunder;

6. penalties, fines, or interest due to violations of contracts, laws, rules, or regulations or due to late payments of taxes, utility bills, or other contractual obligations;

7. costs of environmental remediation;

8. costs of repairs due to the negligence or intentional misconduct of the landlord or its employees, agents, or contractors;

9. advertising, space-planning expenses, legal fees, brokerage commissions, tenant improvements, allowances, concessions, and other expenses incurred in procuring tenants for the property;

10. legal fees, court costs, or other fees or costs of enforcing leases;

11. any costs for which the landlord is reimbursed (whether by insurance or otherwise);

12. cost of repairs, alterations, or replacements caused by casualty losses or other events to the extent actually insured or self-insured against by the landlord or required to be insured against by the landlord pursuant to this lease;

13. cost of repairs, alterations, or replacements caused by the exercise of rights of condemnation or eminent domain;

14. fees or other compensation paid to subsidiaries or affiliates of the landlord for services on or to the property, to the extent that the costs of such services exceed competitive costs of such services;

15. cost of repairs or replacements of any equipment or component of the property caused by deficient design, selection of materials, construction, or improper maintenance;

16. costs relating to maintaining the landlord's existence, either as a corporation, partnership, or other entity, such as trustee's fees, annual fees, partnership organization or administration expenses, deed recordation

expenses, legal and accounting fees, and business, corporation, or franchise taxes;

17. costs for purchasing and installing sculpture, paintings, or other objects of art; and

18. management fees in excess of 3 percent of gross receipts from the property.

Note that capital expenditures are totally excluded in this list. Expect a negotiation on that one.

Special consideration has to be given to the multipurpose office building— a building or complex with retail and office premises, or even residential units. While the language in the leases pertaining to those respective uses might parallel that in leases for a building with only one use, when it comes to pass-throughs, there are special problems to address. Does the assessor assess different uses at different valuations? If so, how is the tax portion of the pass-throughs to be allocated between the portions of the property? Retailers generally clean their own space, so how are the operating expenses allocable to janitor service to be handled? Are there more common areas for the retail space? Are there restaurants causing greater cleanup require-ments in the common areas? How are parking requirements increased and how are the additional costs for maintenance and snow removal to be dealt with? How can tenants avoid double dipping by the landlord in such a complex situation? How can these issues be dealt with directly and with a minimum of special lease provisions? I cannot really attempt to answer the questions because the situations are so diverse, but it is certainly impor-tant to raise the issues.

Retail Leases

Retail leases customarily include the same type of tax provisions that are included in industrial/warehouse leases and in office leases. They might also include operating expenses language (or comparable common-area maintenance expense language) such as was discussed in the office lease section above. That language may partake of the same issues and must be carefully reviewed.

In the situation where there is a freestanding store in an urban setting with no common areas, the landlord may not be providing any services; the tenant may even be required to do snow removal from the sidewalk in front of the store. In that situation, there will be no operating expense or common-area pass-throughs. At the other extreme is the enclosed regional mall with very extensive services rendered by the landlord. Most retail is somewhere between the two.

In the enclosed mall situation, the landlord has a great variety of expenses to pass through to the tenants. The enclosure itself is a vast common area. There is heating and cooling of the enclosed common areas in addition to heating and cooling the various store premises. There may be roof leaks in the enclosed common area and other special maintenance problems. If some of the stores open on the enclosed mall and some do not, allocation of the pro rata share for each type of tenant could present problems because the mall stores will be paying for heating and cooling the mall itself, for extra security, and for extensive cleaning and maintenance. The tenant's broker must confirm that the costs are properly allocated.

Shopping malls, whether enclosed or not, have many common-area costs. If it is in the North, there is snow and ice removal. There is landscape maintenance in the north or south. There is certainly security. There are cleaning crews. Of course, there are costs for general maintenance, repairs, and replacements. Landlords will seek to pass those costs through to the tenants so as to maintain the contemplated net return on their investments. As in other types of properties, tenants will be concerned about quantifying their risks and reducing surprise expenses. They will want to confirm that, in a gross lease with stops, the stops provided for in the lease are really the base expenses, as discussed on page 22.

There may also be outlots on the shopping mall property that participate in some of the expenses and not others.[2] For example, if there is a parking lot shared by the mall and the outlots, how are those costs to be allocated?

---

2. An outlot is an area on the periphery of the landlord's property that is not, technically, part of the shopping mall and is leased or held for lease by a restaurant, a bank, or a similar tenant that needs parking and ready access to the adjoining streets. It may be owned by an unrelated party. Allocation of the various expenses may be governed by a declaration of easements, covenants and restrictions, which will, among other things, allocate costs among the parties.

What if one of the outlot tenants is a movie theater that has parking requirements that are especially large, considering the number of theater seats? The theater has extended hours. The outlot tenant may be a restaurant that has extended hours as well, or it may be a fast-food facility that generates a lot of debris in the parking lot.

Obviously the pro rata share of various tenants may depend on a number of considerations. There is a serious one that may arise in the case of a mall or shopping center with a major tenant, such as a department store, a major discounter, or a big-box operator. That tenant may negotiate a deal under which its contribution to operating expenses or common-area expenses is capped at a level far below what it would be if it were paying its straight pro rata share of those expenses. The rationale is that, since the major tenant creates considerable traffic for the mall or center, the other tenants derive a special benefit from that tenant's being there and, in effect, should subsidize that tenant. It is probable that a more accurate statement of the reason that a major tenant requests that benefit is that it has the economic clout to get it. In either case, giving such a concession to a major tenant means that all the other tenants' pro rata shares are increased, so they are not really in proportion to the rentable area of the property.

As you can see, the base or fixed minimum rent negotiated by the parties (or their brokers) is the tip of the iceberg. It is additional rent, either in the form of financial escalations or pass-throughs, that may determine the real economics of the lease, and as to those, the "devil is in the details."

Energy-Saving Equipment

Although I discussed the issue of including capital expenditures in connection with pass-throughs for various types of properties, the issue of passing through the capital cost of energy-saving equipment is a unique one. Unless the landlord is a substantial user of energy for common areas of the property, such as for an enclosed mall, most of the benefits of installing expensive energy-saving equipment will inure to the benefit of the tenants only. They are the major users of the heating, air conditioning, lighting, and other energy-consuming equipment. Thus, there is what has been referred to as a "split incentive issue." Most people and businesses—including public relations–minded tenants—are concerned about being "green" these days and, frankly, this is the wave of the foreseeable future. Almost all leases that provide for pass-throughs deal generally with capital improvements one way or the other, but most such leases do not yet deal with pass-throughs for energy-saving capital improvements. They will.

The New York City Mayor's Office of Long Term Planning and Sustainability convened a working group of major building owners, tenants, property managers, lawyers, and engineers to address the split incentive issue, and the group developed lease language to allocate the cost of those improvements. Suffice it to say that this is a developing area in commercial leasing of multi-tenant buildings where operating expenses or common-area expenses are passed through to the tenants.

Relocation

Another possible issue—particularly in office leases, although it may also occur in retail or industrial/warehouse leases but not with the same frequency—is the right of the landlord to relocate the tenant to other premises. Landlords want this right to deal with situations in which the location of an existing tenant might prevent the landlord from leasing a substantial amount of space to another tenant. For example, because other tenants have vacated, a small tenant might be the only tenant on a large floor. If the landlord has the possibility to lease the entire floor to a new tenant, it will want to relocate the tenant to another floor in the building, or even to other space in a nearby building owned by the landlord or by an entity related to the landlord. In a retail situation, a new tenant may require certain frontage, which may require the landlord to relocate an existing tenant into adjoining space on the other side, or even to a new location in the mall. The landlord is usually willing, under those circumstances, to pay for the move, even one that is very expensive, if the landlord determines that there will be a substantial net economic benefit to it.

Relocation is very problematic for tenants, even if the landlord agrees to relocate the tenant over a weekend, is willing to pay all the costs, and to minimize the inconvenience to the tenant. The first issue for the tenant is the description of the replacement premises. If the tenant leased its space because it had certain views or was on an upper floor of a multistory building, it would want the new space to have a comparable view or not be on a lower floor. In the retail mall situation, the tenant may have selected its location because of traffic generated by certain other tenants and will be very fussy as to the location of the move.[3] Usually lease provisions dealing with relocation state that the replacement space will be approximately the same size, but are vague on the amount of the variation. If the space is 10 percent smaller, it may not work for the tenant. If it is smaller at all, the rent (and pro rata share) should be reduced. If it is larger, the tenant does not want to pay more rent or additional rent. An issue rarely considered in the landlord's lease is the configuration of the space. Just because a space is the same size does not mean that it will work for the tenant. It might be too long and narrow, or have a vast open area and too little window access. In short, the tenant will want the space to be truly comparable. Finally, there is the issue of what costs will actually be borne by the landlord. The tenant will want the landlord to build out the new space to look like the old one, including decoration and amenities; it will want the landlord to install cabling for all its phones and computer equipment; it will want the furniture, fixtures, equipment, and all of the tenant's other personal property to be moved by a responsible mover that will put the new premises in condition for immediate use. The tenant will also insist that the landlord pay for replacement stationery and other printed materials that had identified the old location.

Relocation does not actually occur very often, because it is very expensive for landlords. However, it does occur occasionally, and the tenant is really entitled to have its operation protected to the maximum extent possible.

---

3. Moving a retail tenant that has already fixtured its store is usually even more expensive than relocating an office tenant.

Measuring the Premises

I have made numerous references to "rentable area," but I have not defined it. It would seem that the definition should be simple, but it is not.

First let me define "usable area," which is the area in the premises that is actually usable by the tenant for the operation of its business. It may include the warehouse and office in the case of a multi-tenant industrial/warehouse lease, the sales, office, and storage area in a retail lease, and the offices, employee lounges, reception areas, and other internal areas used only by the tenant and its employees in an office lease. It is basically the areas that are for the tenants' exclusive use.

The problem arises from the fact that almost all multi-tenant buildings have common areas—areas in the building that are used by more than one tenant and the employees and guests or customers of those tenants, or areas used by the landlord to service the tenants. Typical common areas in an office building, for example, are the lobby, common corridors, restrooms, janitor closets, mechanical and electrical areas, and even the exterior walls of the structure. Since those facilities are for the benefit of all of the tenants, most leases provide that a share of those common areas is, in effect, leased to the tenants. Accordingly, the tenants pay for their usable space plus their share of the common areas, and the total is the tenant's "rentable area." In fact, the area of the entire building that is being divided among the tenants, excepting only vertical penetrations in a multi-floor building (such as staircases and elevator shafts), is included in the "rentable area." The difference between the rentable area and the usable area of a building is now referred to as the "loss factor."

Obviously in the single-tenant situation, the rentable area is the whole building, but even there issues may arise. Assume, for example, that you are representing the landlord in a small, urban single-tenant retail building fronting directly on a commercial street. The structure is designed so that part of the facade is set back from the property line. In that situation, the landlord may wish to make the property line the boundary for the premises and include the setback area in rentable area.

Usually leases merely specify the tenant's rentable area and its pro rata share of taxes and common-area expenses, and tenants just accept that.

However, sophisticated tenants, especially in buildings with large loss factors, sometimes question that or even contest the measurement of their usable area and also how the rentable area has been calculated.

Rentable area issues arise in all multi-tenant leasing situations, but I will focus on office leases as an example:

Let's say you represent a tenant in a 10-story, 300,000-square-foot multi-tenant building that has a loss factor of 4 percent—that is, 4 percent of the building is common area—except that it is now referred to in the Building Owners and Managers Association International (BOMA) standards (discussed in the next section) as the "service and amenity area," to differentiate between traditional common areas and nontraditional amenities, such as conference rooms provided free to tenants (but I will continue to call them common areas). Your client is leasing the top five floors—half the building. All the corridors will be internal, as will the restrooms and other facilities, which are usually common areas. In fact, the only common areas being used by your client will be the building lobby. Should your client's rentable area be equal to its usable area, with an add-on only for the lobby? If its share of the 4 percent is added to its rent, it is seriously overpaying.

On the other hand, let's assume that you represent a tenant on a multi-tenant floor in the lower five stories of the same building, and let's assume that the five-floor tenant did not negotiate the exclusion of what would otherwise have been common areas on its floors. However, the actual loss factor is not 4 percent; it is really 2 percent, plus the lobby (but let us leave that aside for the purpose of this discussion). Under those circumstances, that smaller tenant is overpaying instead.

If you are not familiar with the BOMA measurement standards, perhaps you should be. While it is certainly possible for the parties to a lease to define binding measurement standards for that lease, generally the parties refer to the standards created by BOMA—often without knowing what those standards are. BOMA has developed standards not only for office buildings, but also for industrial and retail buildings and for residential multi-tenant buildings. BOMA also released a standard for multiuse buildings in June 2011. The standards are contained in six books. They are very complicated and are frequently revised. I admit that I am not an expert in those standards, but even if I were, this is not the place for an extended discussion.

The standards can be purchased from BOMA, and BOMA even has "Official Interpreters" to assist in understanding those standards. If you have serious measurement issues, either in connection with representing landlords or tenants, or even if you feel it appropriate to be familiar with them, you can buy the standards. It may, however, be easier simply to consult an architect and let him or her try to figure them out.[4]

Covenants

By covenants, I mean agreements in the lease whereby the tenant or the landlord agrees to perform or refrain from performing certain acts that affect the property or the economics of the property for the other party. Many covenants have already been discussed in Part II of this book. However, there are some covenants that are peculiar to particular leases that I would like to discuss here.

Industrial/Warehouse Leases

A key covenant in many of these leases is the obligation to operate the business only for the permitted use or purpose, and for no other purposes. A careful landlord will evaluate the use and nature of the use of its tenants to make certain that the tenant will not cause unexpected damage to the premises. The landlord may even visit the tenant's prior premises to see how it operates and to make certain that the premises are suitable for the tenant's use so that the tenant will not be asking to make alterations that would make the premises less leasable after the term expires.

Landlords, not surprisingly, are very concerned that the tenant's operations might create an environmental law violation or, more stringently, that the tenant may be using hazardous substances (the tenant, on the other hand, wants to make certain that the premises do not have preexisting conditions that might create a problem for it). The landlord may be concerned about trucks on the parking lot, which may be designed for the weight of automobiles but not for trucks. It may want to know how trucks will be

---

4. The BOMA website for the purchase of the standards is www.store.boma.org.

staged when delivering or picking up goods, whether they might be blocking the roads or standing with their motors running for long periods of time. The lease may prohibit outside storage or, if it is allowed, require fencing or screening. Once the landlord has a good understanding of the tenant's business, it can insert language in its lease to protect itself, such as it tried to do in the stinky fish case I discussed on page 19. Food handling or processing is an especially potent area for covenants because of the possible need for refrigeration, the risk of vermin infestation, and issues of garbage handling and odors.

From the tenant's perspective, the tenant and its broker should examine the covenants in the lease to confirm that they do not actually prevent the tenant from using the premises to conduct its intended business. The space may simply not be suitable for the tenant.

Office Leases

Here again we must take into account what type of office lease we are considering. One of the problems with writing a book of this kind is that both the writer and the reader tend to view a category of leases as something monolithic. Say "office" and we think of a downtown or suburban office building and not of the one-story building, perhaps with a single tenant. Keeping in mind that you may also have to review and negotiate leases for those smaller buildings, however, this discussion will proceed on the assumption that we are dealing with a multistory office building either in the central business district or in an outlying area (the major difference between the two being the availability of on-site parking).

It is difficult to cover all the covenants binding on tenants since the entire lease creates such obligations. For example, tenants are required to comply with applicable laws and ordinances and the requirements of the landlord's insurance underwriters. Tenants may not bring hazardous materials onto the premises. Some of those covenants are particularly acute in medical office buildings, where tenants may be doing x-rays or treating patients with substances that should be safeguarded and not permitted to go into the drains or the atmosphere. Medical office leases tend to have more restrictions than general office leases.

Many of the covenants binding on tenants are those that sometimes find their way into rules and regulations attached as exhibits to leases. Typically, they deal with subjects like prohibiting animals (except service animals), not defacing elevators, closing the corridor door, lettering on entranceways, not raising the landlord's insurance costs, or keeping dangerous materials on the premises. I like to include those provisions in the lease itself rather than in separate rules and regulations (although my lease form permits the landlord to make rules and regulations in the future). Sometimes, however, landlords want many and very specific provisions; in that case, the exhibit format may be more appropriate. In fact, I once reviewed an office lease that had 38 general rules and 11 parking rules (plus 43 rules for contractors attached to the work letter). That, in my judgment, was overkill.

Tenants (and brokers) often ignore a rules and regulations exhibit. That could be a dangerous mistake. The lease probably states that violation of rules and regulations is a default under the lease. That means that those rules and regulations are an integral part of the lease even if they are hidden in the back. There may be rules that are inconsistent with other provisions in the lease—other provisions for which you have negotiated. That creates an ambiguity. They may impose additional obligations on the tenant that were not contemplated by it and that, if they had been in the body of the lease, would have been negotiated out. Treating rules and regulations to be meaningless boilerplate is a very bad idea.

Office leases also impose, or should impose, obligations on the landlord that are extremely important to the tenant—the obligation to provide services. Here is a typical list of services from a lease form I use:

1. Maintenance of the exterior and all structural parts of the building, the common areas, and the parking areas, and the plumbing, sewage, and drainage systems (except the plumbing, sewage, and drainage systems serving the premises only).
2. Heat and air conditioning of common areas during normal business hours, Saturdays, Sundays, and holidays excepted, whenever heat or air conditioning shall, in the Landlord's judgment, be required to maintain comfortable temperature and humidity.

3. Lighting of common areas and parking areas during appropriate hours, depending upon seasons of the year.
4. Snow plowing in parking and exterior common areas.
5. Maintenance of landscaping in the common areas.
6. Window washing of the exterior of all windows in the Premises and the Building, weather permitting, at intervals to be determined by the Landlord.
7. All janitorial and cleanup services (including rubbish removal).
8. Maintenance of all HVAC equipment installed by the landlord.
9. Water for drinking, lavatory, and toilet purposes.
10. Elevator service (which may be reduced during non-business hours or to service the elevators, provided that some service will be available at all times).

It is a nice list, but tenant brokers should be aware of the issues it raises. In 2, what are the "normal business hours"? Normal for whom? What heat and air conditioning will be provided after hours to accountants during the tax season? What is the charge for after-hours HVAC? How much notice will the landlord require to provide after-hours HVAC? Just what temperature will be maintained during the various seasons of the year? What holidays justify turning down the heat; can the landlord do so on Columbus Day, for example? As to 6, how often will the exterior windows be washed? Regarding 7, just what are the standards for the janitorial services and what is the frequency? If the landlord has a contract for those services that specifies what is to be done where, it should be attached as an exhibit, as specifying what the landlord will provide subject, perhaps, to minor modifications.

Obviously all the services are important to the tenant, but some may be more important than others since, without them, the tenant is unable to operate its business. It can live without janitorial service for a week if there is a strike, but it cannot live without elevator service if it is on the 42nd floor. So what happens if vital services are interrupted? There are two situations here: one in which it is outside the landlord's control (such as an interruption of service by a public utility) and the other is caused by the landlord (such as failure to maintain the elevators). As to the former, it may be possible to negotiate a rent abatement if the interruption continues for in excess of a specified number of days. As to the latter, the landlord is in default and the tenant has its remedies in that it can sue for damages, right? Maybe not. Watch for language here that seeks to limit the tenant's remedies to the rent abatement.

Retail Leases

Here is where the parties go really wild on covenants.

Let's start with the landlord's covenants. This is the flip side of the com-mon-area expenses or operating expenses that we were so worried about above. The tenant really wants the landlord to provide the services for which it seeks to charge. In office buildings, with the exception of medical buildings and similar high-volume offices, most of the users are employees of the tenants. While that may be a fairly substantial number of people, it does not compare with the customer traffic at a mall or shopping center. Not only can the center not succeed without that traffic, it cannot succeed if the center is not well maintained and well managed. Good maintenance and management (including security) is critical for the landlord that wants a fully leased center with tenants that can pay their rent, and also wants to collect percentage rent on its percentage rent leases. Even though the landlord and the tenant have a commonality of interest in the services, the tenant will still feel more comfortable if the landlord's obligations are spelled out in the lease.

Many tenants also seek exclusives, which I discussed on page 27. Of course, granting an exclusive to a tenant requires that the landlord keep good records so it does not inadvertently default by leasing in violation of the exclusive. The landlord may also have to insert in all its leases a cov-enant by tenants not to violate those exclusives, which, of course, will have to be disclosed to them.

When we look at the tenants' covenants, we find a very extensive list. First, we may find a restriction on a tenant opening another store within a specified radius. This will apply not only in shopping centers but also as to the freestanding store, because the purpose is usually to protect the generation of sales for percentage rent. Trading areas were alluded to on page 27. The size of the radius will, no doubt, depend on where the store is located. If the store is in a suburban area, the trading area might be five miles because customers usually drive to those centers and it is very easy to drive from one area to another. In congested areas, however, the trading area is usually much smaller since in that situation the customer must take public transportation or park the car in a parking lot or at a parking meter and it is not convenient to travel five miles to another store location. In that situation, a store five miles away is not strong competition, but a store three blocks away is. The shopping center landlord might want a radius restriction even in leases where there is no percentage rent but it is counting on that tenant, as a destination tenant, to generate traffic in the center, and another store nearby might divert that traffic.

Perhaps the most important tenant covenant, however, is what is called the "operational covenant." It is an agreement by the tenant to operate its business in the entire store (except for minor areas for office or storage use) on all days (or on specified days), during specified hours, during the entire term. The landlord wants this principally to assure that the tenant is open so it can have sales on which to pay percentage rent, but landlords in shopping centers may want it even in situations where there is no percentage rent because a dark store in a shopping center is a terrible negative for the center. That provision is often the source of intense negotiation.

Landlords are also concerned about where the tenant's employees park. If the employees park close to the sales area or, in the case of a small center, in front of the store, that makes access by customers more difficult. So the lease may require that the employees park in a designated employee parking area and that the vehicles of employees be identified.

Landlords in upscale malls are also concerned about the quality of merchandise being sold and will prohibit going-out-of-business sales or other sales not in keeping with the quality of the mall. Such leases may also limit sales outside of the premises themselves, except for specified promotions.

In shopping malls, it is not unusual for the landlord to require tenants to participate, at their expense, in promotions or to join a merchants' association.

If the tenant is selling food, there will be special requirements regarding trash storage and removal, as well as extermination. The provisions are even more stringent for restaurant operations, to prevent venting and sewage disposal problems. If liquor is sold or served, the landlord will require that the tenant be properly licensed and, if there is possible dramshop liability in the state, it will require appropriate insurance to protect the tenant and itself from claims or costs.

Conclusion

We are coming to the end, but do not close the book yet. Some important lessons are yet to come!

You may have noticed the frequent use of the word "usually," and also of the words "generally," "customarily," "typically," and "frequently." I am sorry for the redundancy, but there was a reason for it: it is impossible to say that all leases provide for something, because that does not happen. On page 120, I said that all leases provide a base or fixed rent and that all leases provide for the use and occupancy by the tenant. I apologize, but I have to contradict myself—even those are not universally true. A landlord and tenant in a retail lease may agree that the tenant will pay only percentage rent, either temporarily or during the term, either because the landlord is very eager to get that tenant into his center and is willing to take the risk on the rent, or because the landlord expects the sales to be so great that it is willing to take that risk, or because of some reason I cannot even conceive of. Likewise, a tenant may be willing to lease a facility and not occupy it solely for the purpose of preventing a competitor from leasing it, or a landlord's owner may be willing to sign a non-occupancy "master lease" for vacant space as an alternative to a loan guaranty.

So what does all this mean to the broker? It means that every lease has surprises! I have been doing leasing since Lyndon Johnson was the president of the United States. You would think I have seen everything, but every time I review a lease for a tenant, I see something new. Sometimes it is innocuous; sometimes it is really detrimental to my client—sometimes it is so clever that I consider incorporating it in my landlord forms. Further, in representing landlords, I have been working with and revising my forms for my entire career in real estate. Maybe I should have hit upon the ultimate lease by this time, but I keep making changes all the time. In fact, during 2012, I changed my retail lease form 26 times. Granted, many of the changes were suggested by my client's in-house counsel and many were minor revisions, but some were fairly substantial changes resulting from thinking about the issues, or learning of a problem while negotiating leases with the tenant's lawyer and broker, or even from representing a tenant in another retail situation.

There are important lessons for the broker in all this.

First, try to digest the lessons in this book about the various types of premises, the various types of leases, and the various provisions in the various types of leases. After all, that is probably why you have read the book to this point. Keep the book around to use as a reference. And it might help us both if you recommend it to your colleagues so you can talk about the issues discussed. Read other sources about leases to increase your knowledge and understanding. Take courses.

Second, review each lease with which you are involved. If you are the landlord's broker and have used and read the lease form before, be certain that you are advised of any changes made in the form so that you are up to date. Create a comparison from the form used in prior deals so you do not miss anything, and so you can see the business terms more readily. If you are the tenant's broker, read the entire lease. Do not just skim it; your mind may fill in what your eyes gloss over and you might miss some real zingers. Reading a long lease can be tedious, I know, because it often is for me. Do it anyway. That is the only way you can make a real contribution. If you have a question, if you do not understand something, ask the lawyer for your client. Ask a colleague. You may even ask your own lawyer. (I was hired once by a broker client—who was representing a tenant—to read a major lease in a situation where I did not represent the tenant; the broker wanted an independent sounding board on that major lease. In addition, I often answer his questions without charge to help him make deals.) Have a stable of other experts, such as insurance agents or construction people, whom you can call with questions.

Third, stay involved in the lease negotiation. Make certain that the lawyer knows that you want to be a part of the team on behalf of the client. If the lawyer balks, try to encourage your client to make it happen. Try to assure everyone that it is a cooperative effort, not an adversarial one. Always remember that it is the client who must make the decisions, not you or the lawyer. If you have a disagreement with the lawyer about an issue, it should be taken to the client for resolution, but try to present it in a way that does not denigrate the lawyer or make him or her defensive.

In sum, the more you know, the more you can contribute, the more you become an indispensible part of each lease deal and the more successful you will be in your profession. Go for it, and good luck to you!

Index